The Good, the Bad and the Crafty

A Police Autobiography

By Paul Hurley

*To Melissa
From Paul
Enjoy the book,
its all true*

Published by New Generation Publishing in 2022

Copyright © Paul Hurley 2022

First Edition

The author asserts the moral right under the Copyright, Designs and Patents Act 1988 to be identified as the author of this work.

All Rights reserved. No part of this publication may be reproduced, stored in a retrieval system or transmitted, in any form or by any means without the prior consent of the author, nor be otherwise circulated in any form of binding or cover other than that which it is published and without a similar condition being imposed on the subsequent purchaser.

ISBN
- Paperback 978-1-80369-217-3
- Hardback 978-1-80369-218-0
- Ebook 978-1-80369-219-7

www.newgeneration-publishing.com

New Generation Publishing

Preface

'People sleep peaceably in their beds at night only because rough men stand ready to do violence on their behalf.'

That quote is attributed to George Orwell and its meaning is self-explanatory, albeit that the word violence could be toned down somewhat. It could refer to our armed forces who fight to maintain our freedom and therefore give the freedom-seekers the right to criticise them for doing it. Or the more dark and devious ways of our secret services, whose little-known activities protect us from the terrorist threat and, again, give those they are protecting the God-given right to criticise them from their comfortable armchairs.

Then there are the police who in the dark days before the 1984 Police and Criminal Evidence Act behaved in a far more robust manner in their aim to bring the wrongdoers to a rather limp wristed justice system. Of course, I am talking mainly of the Criminal Investigation Department and their method of working.

One could argue that the high-profile miscarriages of justice, together with other criticisms of the legal system led to PACE, and this cannot be denied. But in my limited experience this did not happen very often, and I never saw either high or low miscarriages in my patch, Cheshire. Several people have admitted to me offences that they did not commit for an assortment of reasons, but it never ended in punishment of any kind – I have mentioned some of them in this book.

I was in plain clothes and the CID in the so-called dark days of the 1970s and early 1980s when the demand for a solicitor was not always acceded to. I'm quite sure that robust interviewing preceded these years into the long distant past when the detective dealt firmly with the suspect and the suspect accepted this treatment as par for the course and to be expected if caught or suspected.

In fact, I know it was my experience of the police in the 1970s was with a view to clearing up crime. Prior to this, in the 1950s and 1960s, the police had a better reputation than they do today.

The CID use two separate views of police corruption, the first is crime, theft and the like which is rare and completely unacceptable. The second is a means to an end, in those far off days this involved a clip around the ear, a bit of robust interviewing. Acts that were against the regulations and possibly the laws of assault but were viewed as acceptable to clear crime and obtain admissions.

This book dips its toes into the seedier side of police work and the more serious and heartrending side. Child abuse, murder and the evilness of drug dealing may not sit comfortably with tongue in cheek humour, but it is all in a day's work and without the black humour of the armed forces and the emergency services life would not be quite so bearable.

Introduction

THERE'S NOTHING MORE EXCITING for a new policeman than his first arrest – even if it's just for shoplifting.

My shoplifter was a well-known criminal from the town's underbelly.

'You'll get nothing out of me,' he said defiantly, when I got him to the police station. He looked me up and down, taking in my crisp new uniform and somewhat uncertain actions.

'If you're still denying it, we'd better go upstairs to the CID,' I said.

His demeanour changed, and his cocksure attitude began to wane as I ushered him up the stairs.

Sitting at his desk was a grizzled detective constable, who sadly has long since departed for the CID office in the sky.

'I've locked this bloke up for shoplifting,' I said, 'but he says it wasn't him. The store detective saw him and everything, but he won't have it.'

'Is that right young man?' said the DC. 'You don't want to tell this officer the truth? Well, we'll have to alter that.'

He stood up from his desk, looked out of the window nonchalantly, and then suddenly punched my prisoner hard in the face. The punch knocked him backwards and he came down heavily, cracking his head on the desk.

That's it, I thought, as I looked down at his crumpled body. *My first and last prisoner.*

I honestly thought he was dead.

Meanwhile, the DC had gone back to his paperwork as if nothing had happened.

Just as I was wondering if I'd actually just witnessed that, or if I was dreaming, the prisoner's eyes opened. He wiped the blood from his nose with the back of his hand as I helped him to his feet.

'Are we having this heinous job now?' asked the DC without looking at him.

'Yeah,' mumbled my prisoner, through bruised lips. 'I suppose so.'

I couldn't believe what I had seen. Numb, I took his arm and ushered him back down the stairs where I summonsed him for stealing four cans of Worthington E beer.

In 1974, though, in the days before the Police and Criminal Evidence Act and video surveillance inside every cell, this was normal practice.

I was to enjoy a long career dealing with the funny side of policing, the heart-warming side, and the heart-breaking side. I would help the innocents and the genuinely misguided, and I would ensure that the baddies got their just desserts. Not for me a comfortable beat in the country, a pedal cycle, a book on sheep-dipping and the quiet life through to a pipe-smoking retirement. What beckoned was the CID and then the even more specialised work in the Regional Crime Squad.

I would be working undercover and dealing with drug dealers, murderers, paedophiles, and an assortment of thieves, scallywags, and vagabonds – and, of course, decent, hardworking people in an assortment of circumstances. I would like to start, though, with the part of my police career that I am most proud of – being a key part of the team that changed forever how child abuse victims are treated and dealt with.

The Good, the bad and the crafty

By Paul Hurley

Paul Hurley spent 11 years in the Royal Navy and 27 years in the Cheshire police, retiring in 2002 when he became a writer. He is a member of the Society of Authors and has an award-winning novel, magazine credits and many non-fiction books. He also has a regular local newspaper column.

The book is dedicated to his wife, Rose.

Contents

Chapter One: My New Squad's Horrendous First Inquiry.9

Chapter Two: Questions for Health Secretary Edwina Curry MP 23

Chapter Three: Another shock is revealed 28

Chapter Four: The early days 32

Chapter Five: PC 1633 of the Cheshire Police 35

Chapter Six: First day amongst the good the bad and the Crafty 41

Chapter Seven: I'm allowed out on my own. 43

Chapter Eight: Public Disorder & My CID Aidship 52

Chapter Nine: In plain clothes waiting for a CID post. 60

Chapter Ten: Back to uniform and tutoring a future leader 64

Chapter Eleven: CID at Last & the Ways and Means Act 75

Chapter Twelve: When You Don't Know What to Do, Go for a Drink! 91

Chapter Thirteen: My first real complaint 96

Chapter Fourteen: Fun and games on the Junior CID course 103

Chapter Fifteen: Accused of assault in Liverpool 111

Chapter Sixteen: The Number One Regional Crime Squad 116

Chapter Seventeen: Undercover on a successful drugs operation 122

Chapter Eighteen: Strike day is the operation a success? 127

Chapter Nineteen: Welsh Robbers & 'rescued by Scallys' 134

Chapter Twenty: Good Detective / Bent Detective? 139

Chapter Twenty-One: Back to Uniform with Stripes 146

Chapter Twenty-Two: Dealing With Famous People 153

Chapter Twenty-Three: Back To the RCS & Domestic Upheaval 161

Chapter Twenty-Four: Stolen Porsches, a Kidnapped Child & National News 167

Chapter Twenty-Five: Crafty old blokes and Hide & Seek 175

Chapter Twenty-Six: Chasing the Welsh Nationalists ... 180

Chapter Twenty-Seven: Warrington CID & a Spate of Murders 186

Chapter Twenty-Eight: A Long Interview with a Bizarre Murderer 193

Chapter Twenty-Nine: Suicide and arresting a police officer 198

Chapter Thirty: Back to Divisional CID a nasty assault and an old paedo 207

Chapter Thirty-One: On the Tail of a Nasty Paedophile 214

Chapter Thirty-Two: Police Federation Work and Discipline Duties 222

Chapter Thirty-Three: Deputy SIO on a possible murder & Kidnapped girl 228

Chapter Thirty-Four: Dealing with Rape Victims and Timewasters 231

Chapter Thirty-Five: Putting the World to Rights 238

Chapter Thirty-Six: Guns and Goodbye 246

Chapter One

My New Squad's Horrendous First Inquiry

JUMPING FORWARD A FEW YEARS TO 1994 when I was a Detective Sergeant at Warrington. A temporary compound had been built in the large drill hall, and the Warrington bombing inquiry was controlled from there while we carried on using the Portacabins in the yard. It's amazing how small bits of information, notes and sundry reports can suddenly develop into something serious. My next explosive message was from the DI, Dave Wilcock. It simply asked me to interview a well-known gangster from Widnes, who was alleging abuse at a care home when he was a boy. Ho-hum, more mundane work, I thought. I was very wrong.

I didn't know it at the time but, I was about to start the biggest paedophile inquiry into child abuse in care homes in Great Britain: Operation Granite. I was about to do what had not been done by many police officers and agencies in the past. I was to take the complaint of child abuse seriously – and act upon it.

'11am Thursday 10/2: 'Paul, I've made an appointment for you to i/v a MICHAEL TIERNEY re indecent assault on him 15 years ago whilst he was in Greystone Heath approved school'.

It was a memo from the Detective Inspector, Dave Wilcock – a seemingly routine memo that was to have far-reaching effects and would lead to the setting up of a full-time Paedophile Squad in Cheshire which still exists today. Back then, in 1994, it was a routine job for me. This man, who was now 28, had been to Warrington eighteen months before and had made a similar complaint; it had been dealt with by way of no further action, as there was thought to be insufficient evidence. Michael Patrick Tierney was from Widnes, Cheshire, a well-known member of the criminal fraternity and a particularly violent man who stood 6ft 9in. He had been convicted of many offences in his criminal career, from motoring and drugs to robbery and serious assault. He was regarded as a dangerous, volatile, and unpredictable criminal.

'I've been here before, nothing happened then, and nothing will happen now, I don't know why I've come. You bastards aren't bothered about me.' He scowled at me across the table. Michael Tierney had kept the appointment, and he had brought a woman by the name of Siobhan Monaghan, a drugs outreach worker, with him for support. His very presence was intimidating he was tall and powerful with an aura of fear and the prospect of impending and unpredictable violence. It was like sharing a room with an unknown savage-looking pit bull.

'Listen to him Paul,' said Siobhan, 'he's telling the truth, and he's upset.'

Now it was my turn to speak. I leaned forward and spoke directly into his face. 'Michael, I have never met you before. I don't give a shit about your background, tell me, and I'll listen.'

He then started to talk and had not gone far when this powerful gangster burst into tears and had to be comforted like a baby by Siobhan. I went to get us a cup of tea and on my return started to write out what he wanted to say in the form of a statement.

He now lived with his wife in Thornhill, Dewsbury, and between them, they had five children. Six weeks earlier he had been driving through Widnes and had seen a man by the name of Alan Langshaw walking up the steps to the Magistrates Court with a young boy. Tierney was wanted on a court warrant at the time so did not want to draw attention to himself, and therefore he did not stop. He then went on to tell me his story, which is as follows.

As a child, his parents had physically abused him, and he had trouble with one of his teachers due to his behaviour. As a result, he started a fire at the school when aged about 10 or 11 years and was put into care until the age of sixteen. He was sent to Greystone Heath residential school in Penketh, Warrington and he described it as an 'approved school', but it was a community boys school by the name of Greystone Heath, and he was sent there at the age of twelve. The morning after he arrived, he said that he ran off and was caught by two of the boys and Alan Kenneth Langshaw, one of the care workers who dragged him back to the school by his hair. He said that he was taken into a dormitory and battered by Langshaw. After a while, this stopped, and Langshaw started to cuddle him. He sat Michael on his knee and told him that while he was at the home, he, Langshaw would be like a father. He had to do everything he was told, and things would be easy for him. They sat there for over an hour and during this time he was petrified. Langshaw was brushing his private parts with his hand through his clothes in an apparently innocent way. Tierney was so frightened that he wet himself while sitting on his knee. Nothing else happened for about a week, then Michael did some small thing wrong and was told to go and have a shower and go to bed. After a while, Langshaw came up and sat next to him. He felt his towel and said it was not even wet. Tierney was instructed to go to Langshaw's house, which was attached to the dormitory. Once there, he was told to go and get in the bath. Langshaw said he would go and get him something to eat. At that time, he felt comfortable with him and believed that someone finally cared for him. When Langshaw returned, he soaped him down in the bath and paid particular attention to his private parts and inserted his finger in Michael's anus. When he did this, the boy was asked if he liked it. He lied and told him that he did. Afterwards, he returned to his dormitory room. Two days later, he was again instructed to go to Langshaw's house for a bath and thought he was being friendly. On this occasion, Langshaw soaped him down again in the same way, but the third time Langshaw buggered him for the first time – he was just twelve years old.

Michael had been told that he was pretty, and he felt very alone, he wanted Langshaw to like him and be friendly. In his own words: 'I felt that I had no one else in the world. He told me that he was going to put his penis up my bottom and that it would not hurt. He told me to soap his private parts, and I did. He then put his penis up my bottom. The pain was intense, and I screamed, but he carried on pushing it in and out. I was crying all the time. When he had finished, he pulled it out and cuddled me. He told me that he was sorry it had hurt, but it would not hurt again. After this first time, it became a regular occurrence. I knew it was going to happen because he would be nasty to me for no reason, then he would be nice. So much happened to me during that period. Times and dates are all mixed up. I can remember that at first, he made out that he was my friend, but after a while, he just made no pretence, he just abused me in every way possible.'

Michael outlined all of the sordid ways in which Langshaw abused him. He detailed the things that were done to him and the things that he had to do. He estimated that after that first time, this man sexually abused him almost every day for more than three years until he left at the age of sixteen.

Michael alleged that most of the staff were homosexual paedophiles and had their favourite boys. He was abused in a lesser way by some of the others, but all of the boys knew what was going on. Langshaw would sit in the communal television room at the back with a boy on his knee, and when the others turned around to look, he would say such things as, 'Turn round and watch the fucking telly.'

On occasions, word got out, and the police were informed of the alleged abuse at the school, Michael remembered one day when he was called to the assembly room to find tables with policemen sat at them. Each boy was asked if the staff were hitting them or anything like that. They all said they weren't, as they knew that if they said anything, they would get battered when the officers left. Michael then said the following:

'I have not been the same since these things happened; I am obsessed with watching my children at all times to make sure that they remain safe. I still feel dirty and used; I don't ever want anyone to know what went on. If this is known publicly, I will kill myself. I am prepared to go to court and give evidence but only on the condition that my name is never made public. I have not been able to put my past behind me and never will. I have wanted to tell a psychiatrist what happened and seek help, but I have never been able to. It has taken a lot for me to come and make this statement. When I saw Langshaw going into court with that boy, I knew that something had to be done. He took my childhood from me. I did not have parents that I could turn to. I was alone and could do nothing about what was happening. I know that Langshaw was a total deviant.'

Some years later, when the Jimmy Savile enquiry started, questions were asked about how abuse could happen, and nothing be done about it. In the case of care homes, the children were just not believed if they said anything despite the shocking degree of abuse.

Michael came in again a few days later and made a further statement outlining incidents when Langshaw would get the boys to abuse each other in his presence and a few other similar incidents. This time, he ended his statement with the following:

'I am not homosexual and never have been. I did not want these things to happen to me. I am now 6'9' tall with two of my own children and three of my wife's. People who know me regard me as a hard man in my neighbourhood and I have never wanted my past to come out.'

The next day I went to see the DCI, Mick Holland.

'That's it, boss, what do you think? I'm going to try and trace Langshaw and see what he's doing, it sounds like he still works with kids.'

Mick read the statement. 'This is a hot potato at present Paul, what with the Welsh job, let's make sure we do it right; pull an operation together and then let me have a look.' Mick was a bluff, straight-talking and very experienced senior detective, a man whom I had the greatest respect for – I had to agree with him. The paedophile inquiry in North Wales involving the Bryn Estyn children's home in Wrexham was ongoing and had received a lot of publicity. It was the biggest enquiry to date and what transpired was that we were in the process of setting up, arguably the next biggest! These operations turned the spotlight on children's homes across the country, and what it revealed was not good. We were not aware of this at the time, but it was quite likely that we would have the same result as Bryn Estyn. Accordingly, it had to be dealt with properly. Cheshire already had two enquiries underway into children's homes looking into historic abuse in the county. An operation looking at Danesford Children's Home in Congleton and St Aidan's Assisted Community Home, Widnes, but they were not going well with little in the way of any disclosures.

Now I had a very strong and detailed disclosure, but I needed to put meat on the bones of it, and this could only come with corroboration. I needed other complaints, and I was determined I was going to get them, but where should I start? Greystone Heath was no longer a children's home. It was opened as a Quaker Run Penketh Friends boarding school having been built in 1834. It closed in 1934 and was bought by Liverpool Corporation and was known as The Sankey School until 1947 when it was re-named Greystone

Heath School. In 1973 the school became a Community Home with Education; it was also known as Greystone Heath Approved School. It catered for boys.

Dave Jones was a DC at Risley and had been one of the teams involved in the earlier complaint about Greystone Heath. There had been a few allegations emanating from boys at the school as described above but these came to nothing due to lack of evidence.

'Dave, I'm going to look at Greystone Heath again but this time with success – come and get involved.' He agreed, and I looked for another staff member. Charlotte Legge was a probationary policewoman on attachment to the CID; I commandeered her as the second recruit to my operation. Now for office space. I seized the empty room next to the detective sergeant's office, and we started our investigation. Now we needed an operation name: now names are computer generated but then a name could be chosen with a tenuous link to the operation planned.

'I think Operation Tarzan,' I said. 'Greystone, Greystoke, that is the connection.'

'No,' said Charlotte, 'Tarzan doesn't sit well with paedophiles, it's a macho name, and they are anything but macho. What about 'Granite?'

'Operation Granite sounds alright to me,' I said. 'Greystone, Granite, has a nice ring to it!' The name was born, a name that was to be synonymous with sick paedophilia in the North West and a name that would eventually become known throughout the country in the field of child abuse investigations. It was to become the largest operation of its kind in Britain.

Our first job was to trace Langshaw, but he could be anywhere in the education system, or he could have left it and moved. All good jobs require luck, and we really needed some. We hit the phones and struck gold when we contacted Liverpool Social Services and spoke with Alan Pickering, a senior social worker.

'Thank God someone is taking an interest in this,' said Alan. 'I have lots of intelligence on what went on in these schools, and no one is interested.' He also told us to be careful about who we spoke to as there were quite a few bad apples within the childcare system. We went to Liverpool and met Alan; he was a font of all knowledge as far as paedophiles were concerned and had somehow obtained the registers naming all the boys who went to Greystone Heath. We finally traced Langshaw working as a lecturer at Halton College in Widnes.

While Alan Pickering's information was undoubtedly a massive bonus, we needed another stroke of luck – and got it. The chief constable Mr J Mervyn Jones had seen fit to disband the Serious Crime Squad, and I was given a number of the redundant detective constables to work on the operation. I had already been to St Helen's with Dave Jones to re-interview the lad who had been named in the earlier, unsuccessful, inquiry as having been abused. It was quite obvious that he had, but he would have nothing to do with us. There was an insight into the trouble that we were faced with: it was one thing finding lads who had been at the home but another thing getting them to open up these horrible old wounds. Greystone Heath had now become an old people's home and thanks to Alan, we not only had the names of the boys but those of the staff. It was a good start. My new team was qualified in the use of the major incident filing system known as the Holmes System (Home Office Large Major Enquiry System) it meant that every piece of information could be logged on the computer system from which a 'paper room' was set up. This 'room' generated 'actions' for the staff to do having been drawn from the computer system. The important ones involved tracing the present whereabouts of the ex-residents. Without these, we would not have a job.

I posted on the wall an offer that I would buy a pint for every disclosure that they came back with. Along with this, there had to be ground rules; a lot of boys who have been in care progress to a life in crime which meant, unfortunately, that a lot of the boys we would trace would be streetwise. Under no circumstances could the fact that possible victims may be eligible for Criminal Injuries compensation be mentioned. The last thing I wanted was for the operation to be bogged down with false disclosures. Nothing should be disclosed over the phone, I insisted, or in front of others and anonymity could be and should be guaranteed. Even though these aggrieved were now adults, the rules of anonymity as applied to children still applied to them. Within a week, we had a few disclosures from other boys who had been abused by Langshaw. After I left the operation and the three operations and others were inked under the Granite name, this was not quite so enforced, and it resulted in claims of false arrests and such like. Before the operations were linked, I had lectured their teams on the requirements and the method of operating.

'Can I go and get him now, boss?' I asked Mick 'He is still in the education system, and we've got more evidence now.'

Mick agreed, and we arranged to go to Langshaw's home in Moreton, on the Wirral, on 7 March 1994, to arrest him. I picked my team and prepared for the visit. The Principal of Halton College had been kept informed and was aware of our plans. DC Carl Sheridan was on the operation, and we worked a lot together. Carl was an experienced detective and sportsman. He excelled at most sports and played football for Irlam Town. I decided that he and I would arrest Langshaw while the rest of the team searched nominated rooms in his ground floor flat.

We arrived at the flat at around 8am and knocked on the door. 'Alan Langshaw?' I said to the sheepish looking man, in the dressing gown, peering from the front door of his flat.

'Yes...' I was faced with a pleasant-looking man, younger-looking than his 42 years, with fair hair.

'I am arresting you for buggery at Greystone Heath some time ago. I cautioned him by the rules.

'Oh my God, I don't believe this.'

DC Sheridan said that we had evidence that he had buggered and abused inmates at Greystone Heath when he was a housemaster there some time ago. We walked into the front room with him, and he was insistent:

'Oh my God, I don't believe this, I have only done masturbation.'

He then sat on the settee, pulled his knees under his chin, and burst out crying. He sat there rocking backwards and forwards while the other staff searched his flat. The flat was clean and tidy with nothing in the way of indecent material – we recovered photographs of children, from one of the draws in the living room but none of an indecent nature. While we were there, a single woman living in an upstairs flat came down to see what was going on. She gave the impression of being a friend of his and comforted him in a motherly fashion. We told her what was happening, and she accused us of not doing our homework properly. Alan was a true gentleman and would never hurt a fly, she said. He was not in any sort of relationship with her, she just thought the world of him and was quite satisfied in her own mind that he had never done anything wrong.

This was the opinion of many people that we came across during the inquiry. Langshaw was a very presentable and plausible man. Listening to this woman, I almost doubted that I had got the right man.

He was taken to the police station, booked in and placed in a cell. Later that day I went with Detective Chief Inspector Mick Holland, a senior member of Cheshire Social Services and the principal of Halton College in Widnes to the college assembly hall where we had called a meeting of parents. We sat at a desk at the front. They were told that Langshaw had been arrested for indecent assault upon boys at Greystone Heath in Warrington. They were assured that his time at the college would be fully examined. We were all taken aback by the strength of feeling in the hall. Parents shouted at us.

'You have got it wrong, he's a lovely man!'

'I have total trust in that man!'

'I would trust him with my children anywhere!'

'It's disgusting what you are doing. Why pick on him? His wife has cancer, and one of his children is an invalid, this is out of order!'

Langshaw had surrounded himself with a totally false air of respectability that included the story that he was married with four children, one of the children was disabled, and his wife had leukaemia. He had fabricated a life which was a total lie. Lecturers at the college had even driven Langshaw to Arrowe Park Hospital on the Wirral where they had waited for him in the car park for an hour while he 'visited' his 'sick wife'. Staff, students, and parents had held collections for him and had given him flowers and chocolates to take home to her.

So, we spilled the beans and told the disbelieving audience: he was not married, had no children and lived alone in a flat! We were to learn later that he had indulged in his perverted paedophile activities in a shed and in the staff room on this very site. As recently as the previous week, he had abused a male student from the college in his flat. It even transpired that he was the member of staff responsible for counselling abused students at the college!

The following day, Carl and I prepared to interview him. His legal representative was an ex-police officer, now a legal executive. Alan Kenneth Langshaw told us his story. He admitted many paedophile offences stretching over his long period as a care worker. One thing that I noticed over the interviews was that although he disclosed the most heinous of offences against boys, he held back when it came to Tierney. He admitted abusing him, but he would not admit buggering him, and Tierney was the catalyst in the whole thing. I believed that he was lying, but I couldn't understand why. However, over two days of interviews, Langshaw outlined what he had done. It was a catalogue of systematic sexual abuse.

Langshaw had started his training at around 16 years of age at Greenbank College in Garston, Liverpool, which was at that time a Liverpool Social Services establishment, to qualify as a residential social worker. (The college is still there but is now part of a registered charity). During his time at the college, he had been sent to Greystone Heath as a placement trainee. Also, during his time, if he is to be believed, he was sexually abused by another social worker by the name of Dennis Grain.

Grain was to figure in Operation Granite later, and in 1995 he received a total of seven years at Chester Crown Court, having pleaded guilty to four offences of buggery, one of attempted buggery and fourteen of indecent assault, he received 7 years imprisonment concurrent. He was aged 64 years at the time and had ruined all of these' lives and yet he received only seven years in prison for four offences of buggery when one offence carries a possible fourteen years. What a mess our weak legal system is in. However, in 2016 when Grain was aged 84 years he was brought before the court again regarding historic offences at Greystone Heath and elsewhere, offences that he had not been sentenced for. One of the abused boys had come forward in 2015, hence the further interview.

On April 4th, 2016, he appeared at Chester Crown Court and admitted indecent assault and seven serious sexual assaults and was jailed for seven and a half years and ordered to serve a further year on licence. He later appealed on the 24th June of that year and had his sentence reduced to six years eight months.

But back to Alan Langshaw. This abuse, according to Langshaw, was why he became an abuser. From training, he went to Greystone Heath in 1972 aged 21 years as a member of staff. During that time, he buggered and sexually abused many of the boys. Paedophilia would seem to have been a way of life in some children's homes in those days – although, speaking later to the retired headmaster, he seemed oblivious to what had been going on during his term in office. There was nothing to suggest that he had been involved in any of it, likewise the schoolteachers; the main offenders in all the incidents we dealt with were the social workers and house parents.

In 1980 he moved to St Vincent's residential home, a similar establishment to Greystone Heath only this time he was in a senior position, in fact, he was made Assistant Principal of St Vincent's Catholic Boys Home in Formby, Liverpool, and then Principal. Here the schoolteachers behaved, as far as we knew, with propriety but the residential care workers were, with only a few exceptions, a different breed. The teachers worked during the day and then went home, it was the care workers who spent the nights with the boys and so had more opportunity to abuse them. There were exceptions but, in my experience, not very many during those years. Under Langshaw, systematic abuse was carried out. If anyone complained, it was put down to their background and the fact that they were lying. Even when the police were called, they tended to believe the adults over the children who had in the main come from broken homes. Nothing was done to stop it.

This, fortunately, does not apply now with the inquiry into Jimmy Savile, and similar enquiries have shed the scales from the eyes of the people in a position to make proper enquiries and stop the abusive behaviour. This is because I, and officers like me, took the bull by the horns and acted. (That is the only time that I will blow my own trumpet) Whereas in the past, most complaints had been ignored due to lack of evidence – or rather because the officers concerned just could not be bothered to get off their backsides and investigate the allegations properly! When Langshaw was accused of abusing two boys at St Vincent's he was suspended. It was investigated by the Merseyside Police; a report went to the Director of Public Prosecutions, and it was decided that there was no case to answer, and he was re-instated. The boys had been referred to a Clinical Psychologist and expert in abused children, Mr David Glasgow, who believed that Langshaw had seriously abused them. He contacted Liverpool Social Services, and they completely ducked responsibility, referring him to the Catholic Social Services who were responsible for St Vincent's. He told them that two children had been abused by the principal – Langshaw – and that he should not remain in his post. His expert advice was totally disregarded, and Langshaw was allowed to remain.

Chapter Two

Questions for Health Secretary Edwina Curry MP

THE LOCAL MP, THE LATE ALLAN ROBERTS, asked a question in Parliament about the case, highlighting Mr Glasgow's concerns and another MP took an interest. Mr Roberts' question was answered in the form of a written reply by the then Health Minister Edwina Currie and said:

'Whilst it is recognised that Mr Glasgow's opinions about the alleged abuse were sincerely held. None of the investigations produced any evidence to support his view that Mr Langshaw had been involved.'

We went to see Mr Glasgow in Leeds, and when I told him why we were there, he was near to tears. He described the incident as the worst experience of his career. Two young boys had detailed to him incidents of sexual abuse; his experience and training told him that they were telling the truth, and this was to all intents and purposes brushed under the carpet.

When we later interviewed Langshaw, he admitted that what the boys had said was correct, and the clinical psychologist Mr David Glasgow had been right in his beliefs. The Catholic Social Services had been wrong, and Liverpool Social Services had been wrong. It is only fair to say, however, that sometime later Langshaw was moved sideways and out of contact with young boys. In 1986 he was sent to work as a Catholic Social Services Training Officer in Southport for a year, still without a stain on his character! After this, he obtained employment with Halton College where he resumed his paedophile activities.

After the extended interviews, Langshaw was charged with nine charges of buggery, nineteen indecent assaults and two gross indecencies involving boys under the age of

16 years. These were specimen charges before he eventually came to court when allegations involving as many as 50 boys were disclosed.

As the first of the many paedophiles appearing at Warrington Crown Court during Operation Granite, Langshaw appeared before Mr Justice Scott Baker and pleaded guilty to the 30 charges. He received prison terms of ten years, five years and one year to run concurrently, meaning that he got just ten years in total. Whoopee-do that will really deter people.

In the meantime, the operation went on and now occupied the large compound at Warrington that the bomb inquiry team had vacated. (Of the two incidents in Warrington, the first, an explosion in the Gas Works was detected and the more serious in Warrington Town Centre where two boys were killed, 3 yrs. old Jonathon Ball and 12 yrs. old Tim Parry did not result in an arrest. (The Provisional IRA carried out both atrocities).

I was in charge of the day-to-day running for a while, and then it was decided to amalgamate the other two less successful ongoing enquiries: Operation Bugle, investigating Danesford Children's Home in Congleton, and Operation Emily, looking into St Aidan's Assisted Community Home in Widnes. There was by now a detective inspector in charge of the rather unsuccessful Operation Bugle. As a result of the amalgamation, he would take charge of the joint operation that would be called Operation Granite after my successful one! I was not happy with this; firstly, because I did not fancy working under the officer Terry Oates who sadly has since died (I got on quite well with him off duty but not his leadership style), and secondly, why should my successful operation have to be taken over by the head of an unsuccessful one? I made my feelings known to the DCI Mick Holland, but I suppose that for management reasons, it was the most sensible option. As Terry was a Detective Inspector, and I was a Detective Sergeant, and it was my fault that I had not bothered to study for promotion. I was to remain on the operation as Team Leader for the original Operation Granite.

As we had been successful, and the other operations at that time had not, I was asked to guide their staff when they joined us. It is very difficult getting grown men to detail intimate things that have happened to them as children. It requires a certain type of interviewer using a surfeit of empathy. Disclosure is very important, but not at any cost. On Operation Granite, we went back as far as the disclosures indicated, into the 1960s on some occasions. Some of the work was extremely stressful. I breached my own code of practice one evening when I was about to leave, and everyone else had gone. The phone went, and it was an ex-resident of Greystone Heath. One of the team had visited him and left a Pro-forma notice through his door, telling him nothing but asking him to contact the police on the given number. The conversation went something like:

Him: 'What do you want to see me about?'

Me: 'There's nothing to worry about, we just need to have a word with you, but would rather it be in person.'

Him: 'Oh come on, I'm a long-distance lorry driver, and I am going to Iran at 3 o'clock in the morning for three months, you can't have me worried about what I am coming back to for all that long, what have I done wrong?'

Me: 'Well nothing, you have done nothing wrong; did you go to Greystone Heath?'

Him: 'Oh that, I know what that is about, it's that abuse thing, isn't it? Well, I was in the football team, and if anyone touched me, I would sort them myself.'

Me: 'That's fine then; the lads will come and see you when you get back and get a negative statement if that's alright?'

There was a short pause.

Him (starting to cry): 'They did the dirty bastards, they did abuse me, I was trying to put it behind me, shit, why does this have to come out now.'

I then had to calm him down as best I could over the phone and then he had to go away for three months, knowing what he had to come back to. I had instructed the teams never to discuss the operation over the phone, just face to face. It was a difficult phone call!

It was very stressful at times, both for the lads and the officers investigating their abuse. I did not have much to do with the investigation into Dennis Grain, but I went on one unpleasant inquiry to see a lad who he had abused at another school, where he was a housemaster! The lad we spoke to had bravely gone and told the headmaster what had happened, and the headmaster had not believed him. As a result, during assembly in front of the whole school, the boy had been made to apologise to Grain (who was also on the stage) for 'telling lies' about him. He then received a public beating for lying about one of the teachers. This was the atmosphere in many children's homes (although this wasn't one, it was a public school!) at the time and was the reason that few complained. As mentioned earlier, there was a difference between Teachers and care workers, but the resident housemaster Grain was believed rather than the student.

On another occasion, during the enquiries, I went to Dartmoor Prison to see Mr Stephen Roderick Norris who, with Peter Norman Howarth, was the main man in the extensive and groundbreaking investigation into Bryn Estyn, the children's home in North Wales. Norris had been the senior housemaster. This was the precursor to the many enquiries that followed. Norris had learned his trade at Greystone Heath before moving to Bryn Estyn, where he was involved in the evilest paedophilia imaginable. When I entered Norris's room in Dartmoor and saw a grey-haired old man sitting facing me, he could have been anyone's grandfather; but I could taste the evil in the room. There was no danger to me, but I knew instinctively that this man really was evil personified. He had a 'presence' that did not require words. I was hoping to speak about paedophile rings with him, but he would tell me nothing. At no time did we find any evidence of a paedophile ring

Chapter Three

Another shock is revealed

Despite Michael Tierney telling me that no one must know of his disclosures, on the first day at court, he was happy to sit on a bench and have a television company interview him. No hidden face, no cover-up and he came over quite well. I think at that time he used a false name.

After Langshaw was sentenced, journalist Allan Urry came to the incident room and asked if he could do a half-hour documentary on the operation. The DI, Terry Oates put the request to the chief constable's office, and the request was denied. What a pity, I thought, it wouldn't do any harm, quite the contrary. The police would come out of it well. Allan had already obtained some footage, filming the incident room and the outside of the police station.

'Allan, do you really want to do this?' I asked after pulling him to one side.

'Yes,' he replied, 'it would make an excellent piece.'

'Well, let's do it then, I'll help you. I can give you nothing that you could not get elsewhere if you knew where to look, and nothing confidential, let's go.'

I took him to the cells, and we filmed gates being slammed, the inside of the cells and tape recorders being switched on. I got him permission to film in the old people's home that had previously been Greystone Heath, and I contacted Tierney and some of the boys we had interviewed and who had been abused. We also had a good rapport with them.

'Do you fancy going on the TV in silhouette, no one will identify you?' I had no trouble in giving Allan a few names to contact, and the programme was prepared, on one night alone. I spoke to Allan from home for an hour discussing and planning the proposed documentary and, on my advice, he featured Mr David Glasgow and allowed him to tell it as it was.

Meanwhile, the DI Terry Oates was not aware that anything was going on! Mick Holland, had he known, would probably have told me to be careful but I know that he would prefer not to know. He was a Detective with a big 'D'. A real one!

On the night that the programme went out as a BBC Close up North - Special Investigation, I watched and taped it. The following day, I went to the office to find the DI Terry Oates full of praise for it. He couldn't understand how they had traced the lads and how such a good job had been done without official permission. Tierney had of his own free will appeared in person but filmed from the back. This was used as the basis for a full Panorama special Hear No Evil on the 10th March 1997 that was cleared by the chief constable.

I had kept in touch with Michael Tierney for a while and visited him, his wife and children at their home in Thornhill, Dewsbury, Yorkshire. The house was a large council house on an estate, I was still not happy to be in his presence. Although he had provided the information to start what is now a full-time Paedophile Squad, all did not seem right. What he had said about Langshaw had, in the main, been corroborated by the man himself but some things Langshaw just would not corroborate – and to be honest, I found myself believing him. On visits to Tierney's home, his children, both boys and girls, seemed fine. He constantly told me in that macho way gangsters have just what he would do to anyone found messing with them. He seemed very protective and once again stressed that after what he had gone through, he could not let them out of his sight.

In 1995 I learned that Tierney had been involved in the first case of 'trolley rage' in the country when he assaulted another shopper. He received 28 days in prison. Back then, I thought it was a bizarre and rather funny story though what I was yet to learn about him was far from funny.

Throughout the time I had been dealing with Tierney, there had been tears and heartrending disclosures, mixed with bravado – an understandable mix of extreme emotions. Horrifically, when I had given him a shoulder to cry on, and when everyone had given him sympathy and support, he had himself been carrying out the sick, systematic, and serious sexual abuse of children both girls and boys from the age of seven upwards. He had done to children everything that Langshaw had done to him and more. And this to the children who were in his house when I visited, children that he was stepfather to were buggered by him, a friend of his stepson whom he sexually assaulted on a camping trip. From the age of 7 years, his stepdaughter had been abused by him moving from masturbation to oral sex to rape up until the age of ten years. He was also sentenced for physically assaulting his stepson.

When he appeared at Bradford Crown Court, he received a longer prison sentence than Langshaw, fifteen years at the last count. But the evil story of Tierney does not end there. He was released from prison on licence after serving about half of the fifteen-year sentence. Soon after he was sentenced to a further 18 months in prison for molesting a young boy. He was released after nine months on licence and sent to Linden Bank Hostel in London Road, Elworth, Sandbach. Protestors complained about having this evil 45-year monster in their midst complaining that Sandbach had become a dumping ground for the nation's perverts.

The story does have a happy ending though because Tierney moved from Elworth to Cinnamon Brow, Warrington where he died of a drugs overdose.

I suppose that he is a perfect example of the theory that some abused children go on to be abusers themselves. If this is what happened in this case, then Langshaw has even more guilt on his shoulders. Even more, innocent young lives have been destroyed because of his activities and the activities of his kind. Tierney, who saw me as one of his true friends, was one of the worst types of child abuser. I just hope that after I left the inquiry, there were no miscarriages of justice when disclosures were made falsely to gain compensation. I know that I dealt with Langshaw, and he was guilty. He was the first to admit it and to date one of the only ones to admit his guilt in court.

I am proud of Operation Granite, of the good that it did, of the evil men that were taken off the streets. Along with everyone involved, I learned a lot of lessons, and as a result, laws and procedures have been implemented to protect vulnerable children. We can, however, never relax in the constant aim to prevent crafty and persistent abusers from being put into a position of trust where children are concerned. When he came forward I never for one minute suspected that the macho Michael Tierney was anything but a rough diamond and to find out that he was himself an evil abuser shook me. He is also an excellent example that no one can be trusted, and society must always be on guard.

Now though let's rewind to my time before I joined the police and began working among the Good, the Bad and the Crafty folk of Cheshire and elsewhere.

Chapter Four

The early days

'JUST SO'S I KNOW, fella, what name did ye give?' The man addressing me in that raw Irish brogue was a rough, middle-aged Irishman with hands like hams.

'I gave my own,' I replied, innocently.

The rough engine drowned out my words, and I choked on the blue smoke from his rusty exhaust. He peered down from the dumper truck, a look of disdain on his weather-beaten face. 'What's that? I can't bloody hear ye!'

'I said I gave my own name when he asked me.' The final four words were shouted across the site as the truck's engine was suddenly switched off. A motley gang of labourers peered over from their digging in the white, fossil-rich clay.

The distinguished old Irishman was Stan, and he had the rank of 'Ganger.' We were on the site of one of the bridges on the new M27 motorway at Fareham in Hampshire. This was my first day as a building site labourer after spending eleven years cosseted from civilisation in the Royal Navy.

'Well, you're a prick, what are ye!' he said. 'No one gives their own name around here. They'll catch up wit' you and ye'll drop us all in the shit.'

It was February 1974, I was 27 and I had joined what was then known as 'the lump' – a dedicated band of construction workers who were paid by their company and then received an additional bonus, care of the government's munificent DHSS office when they signed on for unemployment benefit halfway through the week. It was all alien to me but accepted by many. Whilst still in the Royal Navy, I'd been accepted for the Cheshire Constabulary, and had been given the number 1633, but with a month to wait I was sampling the heady civilian life. I'd had a go at working in a TV factory for a week – mindlessly boring – and now this.

I'd joined the Navy just after my sixteenth birthday, so had little experience of 'normal' life. It was a different world, especially initial training. Each class had its own instructor, and all branches of the service were mixed in together. The petty officer instructor treated his charges abominably, but the drill instructor or GI (gunnery instructor) was even worse. He smoked and shouted non-stop, and his voice was like a ton of gravel sliding off a truck.

My mind drifted back to my first months in the service. Once a week, the man known as the Sky Pilot, the God Botherer, the Bish, or, more formally, as the ship's padre, would visit each department in turn to say a few prayers. On this particular day we had all been sent into the drill shed to await his arrival. When we got there, a few lit up their cigarettes and, just before the padre arrived, the Chief GI walked in, complete with black canvas gaiters, black canvas belt with gleaming chrome buckles, and a long whistle chain.

He was immaculate. The reflected light shone from the crossed gold lace guns on his lapel, and the peak of his cap touched his nose. From beneath it, his small, piggy eyes surveyed the room malevolently. I caught the sweet smell of rum. Suddenly his mouth opened wide, and his southern voice boomed out. 'What are you cants doin' smoking in 'ere? Donchew fackin' know this is the aase o' fackin' gawd? Put 'em aat an' 'ave a bit o' fackin' respect, yew shower o' cants!'

The padre – a lovely man, doubtless the youngest son of Lord somebody or Admiral so-and-so – arrived for the tail end of the speech and stood there, beaming. He was used to flowery Naval talk of this type; I was yet to become inured to it.

I suffered the usual traumas of a new boy. In the afternoon we had tea, which usually consisted of Sunny Spread (a honey substitute) and bread, issued to each rating by one of the cooks. On one occasion I was still hungry and, like Oliver Twist, went back for more. Unfortunately, the duty petty officer overheard me committing this serious breach of Naval etiquette and called me over.

'You greedy little bastard, what are you?'

'A greedy little bastard sir,' I replied, lowering my head.

'You're nothing more than a shitehawk, what are you?' Shitehawk' is Navy slang for a seagull.

'Nothing more than a shitehawk, sir.'

'And where do we see most of the shitehawks, boy?'

'Out at sea, sir.'

'Out at sea? Out at sea?! How the fuck would you know that? You've never been there. How would you know what it's like at sea?'

'No sir, sorry sir,' I gabbled. 'I did go on the Mersey ferry once, and there's shitehawks there.'

I was trying to be helpful, but it sent him into orbit.

'The Mersey fucking ferry?!' he screamed, his face bright red, veins popping in his neck. 'The bins lad! Shitehawks are always stealing from the dustbins! That is where you belong!'

I spent the rest of the afternoon – at his request – standing in the filthy dustbin outside the front door, flapping my wings and shouting, 'Squawk, squawk, I'm a shitehawk, squawk, squawk, I'm a shitehawk.'

I never asked for any more Sunny Spread.

Men like the duty PO and that old GI – long dead, I'm sure, probably from throat or lung illness – would now be called bullies. It *was* bullying, I suppose, but it was for a purpose. It took boys and turned them into men. We feared him as we feared God himself, but by passing-out time 'evil' men like him had become father figures, and we competed to buy their pints and shake their hands.

They guided me into an eleven-year career in the world's greatest navy – and I could write a whole other book about what went on there – but after circumnavigating the globe several times I ended up with a wife and two young children, and the need for a more stable life.

Chapter Five

PC 1633 of the Cheshire Police

Brenda and I moved to the Cheshire town of Winsford in February 1974 with our son Mark and daughter Andrea, then four and three respectively, and took up residence in a police house. Shortly after moving in, the previous occupant visited in his uniform – I must admit to being a bit in awe, never having had a policeman in my house before. He was a strange chap, whose do-it-yourself projects I spent the next year putting right. Like the coal fire with the glass door which gave out no heat whatsoever and was not connected to the boiler properly, so that it served no purpose whatsoever other than being a dumping container for expensive coal. Then there was the soak-away that he built in the garden to take the waste water from the garage roof. This had been dug into the solid clay of the area, so was as porous as a soup plate; every time it rained the garden flooded. It was only when I started at Winsford police station that I learned that his unique way of working was not confined to DIY.

Until then, like most good-living, law-abiding Catholic boys, I had put the police on a pedestal. They were frightening and official. They were good, and sensible and caring, and they never did any wrong. I was about to find out how wrong this assumption was, and how crumbly the pedestal.

This officer crashed his car into a lorry, left the police due to his injuries, met a travelling preacher, followed him around the country, found God, recovered, and was let back into the police. Soon afterwards, he found that his wife was having an affair, drove to the lover's place of work, in uniform, and gave him a thump. He then left the police a second time. A true eccentric if ever there was one.

I spent a week on an induction course at the Force Training Centre at Crewe, where I had the thrill of donning my full police uniform for the first time. Despite us being the boys in blue, it was black with silver trimmings, and in Cheshire it did not include a whistle. There was, however, a secret pocket for my small wooden baton; that baton would later come in handy for cracking nuts, bashing wild dogs, and breaking windows. (Policewomen had a half-sized one – presumably because they only hit small people and little dogs.) I was also issued with a set of handcuffs, and I soon invested in a leather handcuff pouch so that I could wear them on my belt, rather than carry them in my pocket or tuck them down my trousers.

Like everyone else in the class, I travelled home with my uniform hidden under a civilian coat, but my peaked cap on the back window shelf of my car for all to see – something officers would not dare do now if they wanted the glass to stay there. My pay on joining was £1,353 *per annum* (for women, the starting pay was £1,287, so that has changed for the better).

Training continued at Bruche, the No1 District Police Training Centre at Warrington, and I soon felt right at home. The Navy is one closed shop, and the police was another and, back then, more so than now, it was run along military lines. We called the course sergeants Sir, or Sarge, and some found it hard to deal with. While my fellow trainees were moaning and groaning about their rooms and the food etc, I thought it was marvellous; I was quite used to institutional grub, and I'd never had my own room before. I achieved top marks in the two most difficult weeks, and the only area where I remember struggling was drill – carried out under the eagle eye of Sergeant Smythe, a Cheshire sergeant and a drill instructor of the old school – all bristling moustache, slashed peak reaching down to his nose, and broad red sash across his chest. The police march in the Army fashion, whereas the Navy style is more like an organised walk, so I had to learn all over again.

The training was first class, both in the classroom and on the 'street' where practical instruction was given. It was designed to prepare you for all that life would throw at you – the instructors played drunken motorists, fighters, wife-beaters, and all the other types you find on the streets of our towns, and always took great delight in vomiting a mixture of breakfast cereal and milk all over your clean and pressed uniform! We learned a fair bit of law, and how to apply it, along with the craft of policing – from recognising and catching criminals to more mundane stuff like dealing with the public and marshalling traffic. Modern concepts like equality and diversity training were barely mentioned. Why would we need them? As police officers it was our duty to treat everyone the same. This applied whether they were black, pink, or one-legged (though it didn't apply to homosexuals, as that was still illegal). There must have been some racism, but hand on heart I never saw or heard any. As in the Navy, there were few black recruits – but those who joined were mates and co-trainees, and their skin colour was totally irrelevant.

At the time the country was on high alert because of the IRA. Night leave was cancelled, so we entertained ourselves in the college. Women were allowed in from outside for the weekly disco to augment the trainee policewomen, who didn't join in such large numbers back then (our class, we only had three). The favourite place to take amenable females was behind the baths, and it was in that location I first realised again just how crumbly the pedestal was. But I was a married man, so I never got up to all that rudeness, I was just told about it.

After twelve weeks at Bruche, it was time to leave. There was a formal dinner, with dinner suits hired for the night, and the following day our families attended for the passing-out parade. Brenda and the children Mark and Andrea, came, we enjoyed a buffet lunch and a speech by the commandant, and then it was home for a few days off before starting at my new station as a probationary constable.

The training had been so good that I felt different. I'd frequently been in charge of Naval patrols, scouring the back streets of various ports for errant sailors; that had been strong arm stuff, with plenty of violence. I'd always been sure I could handle anything that the streets threw at me; but now I knew I could do it within the law.

Winsford was quite a busy town of some 35,000 inhabitants which had recently accepted a large influx of overspill residents, mainly from Liverpool, but some from Manchester. Many of them did not work, even when there's work available. And thousands of these 'problem families' moved in and occupied three recently-built council estates. The houses were crowded together with footpaths between, in a way unique to the mad modern town planning prevalent in the 1960s and 1970s. The architects of these concrete jungles invariably won awards for their 'groundbreaking designs', but in fact they had built greenhouses to nurture anti-social behaviour and domestic breakdown. Sadly, they also housed lovely people who had moved from the city and tried to keep themselves to themselves.

The main estate was called Mount Pleasant and to the decent residents – and there were a large number of law-abiding, low-paid families living there, at least initially – it was anything but. Every bad tenant the council had trouble with seemed to be sent our way; over the years, many of the respectable folks would escape, leaving the unfortunates who could not get out to their fate as the lowlife took over. I always found it so sad to walk through these estates and see clean and well-kept houses dotted around amongst the rusting fridges, old cars, and boarded-up windows. It affected the decent people in unseen ways, too.

'Hello, Mr Electrical Retailer. I'd like a washing machine on tick, please.'

'Certainly, what's your address?'

'Er, Mount Pleasant.'

'Sorry, we don't do credit for people from there.'

So, the Council had a brilliant idea. Why not change the name from Mount Pleasant to The Over Estate and create nice names to make them look like real streets and avenues? This was done, at great expense.

'Hello, Mr Electrical Retailer. I'd like a washing machine on tick, please.'

'Certainly, what's your address?'

'Er, Cotswold Way.'

'Sorry, we don't do credit for people from there.'

Twenty years after I joined, common sense would prevail. Many of the houses were knocked down or thinned out, and many of the problem families were relocated. Now the area is somewhat more respectable.

The town was split into two for policing purposes, with Panda 6 at one end and Panda 7 at the other. The Panda 7 end encompassed the new, precinct-type town centre and the rougher estates. At this time, 1974 the main A54 ran through the centre of the town on what was quite a narrow route, until it was turned into a dual carriageway-cum-rat run, which really did split the place in two.

Like all probationers, I first had to spend four weeks with a tutor constable. Mine was PC Pete Gaskell, a sound, professional, and laid-back officer with some three years' service. A touch old-fashioned, he tended not to mince his words. As my car was off the road for some reason, he picked me up in his antiquated Triumph Herald. My first duty was nights, 10pm to 6am. I was brimming with self-confidence and could not wait to get amongst the action.

'I always work Panda 7,' said Pete as we went for the briefing. 'Get yourself a radio.'

I selected a Philips Pocketfone radio and inserted the little yellow re-chargeable batteries, stuffing the receiver into the top of my tunic. The transmitter with the pop out aerial I put in my pocket, as the duty sergeant outlined the current state of the section. We went through recent arrests and suspects, information that had come in, and the sergeant finished with a few strange things called 'Express Messages.' For these we had a little pink note book and a little yellow one for the different type of message. We laboriously transcribed these messages as dictated by the sergeant. Some of it was of interest, but much of it was about wanted people and missing vehicles from the other side of the country. I never understood why we wasted most of the parade writing them into our little booklets. I never once looked at them out on the street.

Chapter Six

First day amongst the Good the Bad and the Crafty

With that done, I was off on my first patrol. Police officers today have a massive workload; they come on duty and the limited time that they have on the streets is spent ploughing through jobs – jobs that then keep them in the police station for even longer. Back in 1974 it was all very different, certainly in sleepy Winsford. We could spend several nights without a call, to the point where we looked forward to the weekends when the Mr Smiths nightclub would be open, and we could expect a fight or an arrest. My colleagues and I enjoyed a bit of aggro, and a punch-up was almost always welcome. It gets the adrenalin going and, to be fair, most males also enjoy it; it's just that we could do it legally, whereas you would be locked up. You don't want to be hurt, but you're quite convinced it will never happen to you, and at 6ft I felt reasonably confident. I'm sure today's officers, respect for the uniform long gone, feel different.

We tended to take a long refreshment break in the early hours, when extended games of cards would take place. After that, the panda drivers would have a quick run around the patch and then park up somewhere for a kip. I soon learned that most of the shift was spent either driving or walking on your beat; there was little of today's endless paperwork.

It was all mundane stuff at first, but a few nights into my first week with Pete the radio passed what sounded a routine message.

'Panda 7, can you go to the White Lion in Delamere Street, the licensee wants some customers to leave.'

Fresh from training, I knew that the licensee could eject anyone from his pub in the same way as a householder can ask you to leave his house. We were there to assist him if necessary. My adrenalin was up as we arrived at the pub, but inside all appeared quiet.

The landlord met us at the door. 'Thank goodness you're here, lads,' he said. 'It's them three. Can you get them to leave?'

I looked over. Three young blokes were sitting at a table in the bar.

'You need to tell them to go,' said Pete.

Sighing, the licensee went over to them. 'Now come on lads,' he said. 'I've told you once, I want you to leave.'

The first said, 'Okay, boss, we're going.'

The second then stood up and punched the licensee hard in the face without warning, causing him to fall backwards and smash the glass in the door with his head.

I then had my first punch-up in the police – well, my first arrest using the minimum force necessary.

My radio flew out of the top of my tunic and shot across the bar. The person I was 'arresting' fought like mad and at one stage I was left holding his jacket as he struggled free. I rugby-tackled him and a few tables and glasses went flying covering us with beer and cigarette ends. Eventually, I had him under control and handcuffed. When everything had quietened down, I went over to get my radio from its respectable rescuer who was sitting at the bar.

'My lad was thinking of joining the police,' said the radio rescuer, indicating a pale and trembling lad at his side. 'Isn't that right son?'

It was obvious that the son had instantly given up any such idea.

Chapter Seven

I'm allowed out on my own.

AFTER MY PERIOD IN COMPANY, I was allowed out on my own for the first time – my big helmet sitting proudly atop my head, and my Navy flightdeck boots on my feet.

It was six o'clock in the morning and most sensible people were still in bed as I strolled out into the mean streets of Winsford.

Next door to the police station was a newsagent, and I was in luck. Parked outside was an articulated lorry and the engine had been left running! My expensive training at Bruche had not been wasted. I knew as soon as I saw it that the driver was committing the offence of 'Quitting' under the Road Traffic Act 1972 – the swine! Didn't he realise that if it slipped into gear, it could wipe out an old people's home or a convent – had one been there? Wasn't he aware of his duties as an HGV driver?

Pulling myself up to my full height, I took out my little process booklet and started to fill in the details. Then the driver came out. He was clutching a *Daily Mirror* and twenty Embassy No6, and his face fell when he saw me.

'Sorry officer,' he said. 'I only nipped in for a paper. What's the problem?'

'Your engine. It's running.'

'Er, yes.'

'Well, it's an offence to leave a vehicle with the engine running and I'm reporting you for it.'

Trying to look like a policeman in *Z Cars*, I didn't look at him, I just kept writing in a suitably officious manner.

'I'm going to caution you. You're not obliged to say anything, but if you do… er, you will… might… er… go to court… er… it will be given in writing and… er, you know what I mean.'

He looked thunderstruck. 'If I get reported, I'll get the sack,' he said. 'How am I to feed my kids then?'

The feeling of pity rose in me and, combined with the fact that I had made a total pig's ear of the caution, melted my resolve. 'Alright,' I said. 'But don't do it again.'

His face lit up, and he was so excited getting up into the cab that he dropped his *Daily Mirror,* and the pages blew down the high street like white birds, settling gently in people's gardens. With a blast of blue smoke, the wagon set off, a highly grateful driver at the controls.

You couldn't let too many people off like that, mind you. The only way a probationary constable could be judged was on the amount of work – called 'process' – that he or she submitted.

I toddled off down the street, trying to remember to walk like a copper, and before long it was time for refs.

The main job of a probationer on the 6-2 shift was to call in at a friendly butcher to buy (for the extreme bargain price of ten pence) enough sausage, egg and bacon to fry up back at the nick. Today this would be called police corruption, as would the free cups of tea that we got from the local cafés.

An uneventful week followed, and then a week on the 2-10 shift – which dealt with domestics and accidents – and finally a week on nights rolled around.

Nights on foot patrol were totally different from nights in a panda, and more than once that first winter I pondered what I was doing. Trust me, it's not much fun walking through a council estate in freezing rain at 3am. If I was lucky, I'd find myself near one of the many abandoned cars on the estates and would huddle in the back seat in my heavy overcoat, trying to keep warm as the hoar frost settled all around me. There was nothing pretty about it as you sat in a derelict Ford Anglia, looking through what was left of its windows at the slab-sided wall of a council house, closely surrounded by old bursting settees and overflowing bins. The sweet smell of cat piss and neglect assailed the nostrils and was only offset slightly by the moon glittering through the fluffy white branches on the trees. In my case, it was made even worse by the memory of doing essentially the same job a few years earlier in places like Miami, Yokosuta and Sydney.

As well as sleeping I did sneak around looking for business, and that was what brought about my first 'Case Dismissed' court case. I was walking through a car park in the early hours when I saw a car with a tax disc for another vehicle in the windscreen. The side doors were locked, but I managed to get in through the tailgate, crawl through the car and triumphantly slide the offending disc from its holder. I traced and interviewed the car owner who, under my careful questioning, soon made a full confession. His story was quite simple; the disc had come from a mate's car, and that car had been scrapped. He told me how sorry he was and assured me that it would never happen again.

What a simple job! Were they all going to be like this?

I stuck my evidence in the summons booklet and sent it to the DVLC, which authorised proceedings. I submitted it as a 'Fraudulent use of Vehicle Excise Licence.'

No need for me to attend court here, I thought. My man would simply plead guilty.

Unfortunately, he went to see a solicitor and decided to fight it.

In the witness box I learned my first lesson about solicitors' devious tricks.

'You say in your evidence that you recovered the disc from my client's car,' he said, innocently. 'Is that correct, officer?'

'Yes, sir,' I said, looking knowingly at the dour magistrates.

'You said that it was in his car, and that you climbed in and got it out. Is that correct?'

'Yes, sir,' I replied again, looking at the magistrates with a touch of condescension on my face.

'But my client says that the tax disc was on the floor of his car where his friend had accidentally dropped it,' said the solicitor. 'What do you have to say now, officer? I will ask you again. Was it *on* his car or *in* his car?'

Now it was the turn of the solicitor to look self-righteous.

'It was *on* his car,' I said, slightly less cockily.

'But you didn't say that did you, officer?'

The offender smirked broadly in my direction, and the magistrates continued to look dour. It took them ten minutes to dismiss the case.

This was a good lesson, and I learned it well. During the following twenty-eight years, over hundreds of arrests and court appearances, I only ever lost one other of my cases in the witness box. Police officers should never assume that solicitors (or barristers) are there to behave fairly and in the interests of justice. Their interest is their client's interest, and that's where it ends.

Back out of the court, for more routine patrolling. Much of what we did then has long since been consigned to the history books. On foot patrol, constables had physically to check the doors on the commercial premises and shops on their beat. In Winsford town centre, that could take most of the night – especially as you had to do it twice, once before and once after 'refs.' If a door was found unlocked, the following day a report had to be submitted to the chief superintendent explaining why. At this point, I must mention my esteemed inspector. He was famous before I joined for many reasons. Out of work he was an excellent chap with a great sense of humour; in work, he could appear very sour and officious, and everything had to be done the correct way – his way. He visited me one night near to the Civic Hall in Winsford and started to walk back the way I had come. We paused by some waste ground, and he pointed across it to the rear windows of a building.

'Have you checked those?'

'No sir,' I said. 'I don't know what's under all that grass.'

'That's stupid,' he snapped. 'You *must* check *everywhere.*'

At that, he strode out over the wasteland and through the knee-high grass towards the windows. Halfway there he disappeared into a deep manhole which was hidden by the grass. I followed him, gingerly, and helped him, mucky and soaking wet, back out of the hole.

After much harrumphing, he composed himself. 'I suppose on this occasion you can give them a miss,' he said. 'In future though…'

He walked off, trailing muddy footprints.

Around that time, 1975 there was a petrol shortage, during the 1970s the country jumped from one shortage of oil to another, wars, Arabian supplies etc. Panda cars were restricted to twenty-five miles per shift. Given the area we covered this was nowhere near enough; Bobbies being inventive types, many a panda car was to be found driving backwards around the industrial estates in the early hours, achieving the dual goal of checking the factories *and* winding the mileometer back. I saw more than one with the driver asleep, back wheels propped up, running in reverse gear. If the driver timed it right, the miles would be right for going off duty when he woke up.

As with everything else, our inspector took this petrol shortage seriously and would walk from Northwich to Winsford to visit us, a distance of some seven miles through the countryside. He would arrive just before we were going off duty at 6am, sign our pocket books and then get the early morning bus back to Northwich. But his rules were there for a reason, and sometimes they worked. When a child went missing from home, officers should search the child's house. This could annoy the parents, who felt slighted not to be believed. Hence, if the parents looked genuine, that inquiry was sometimes missed out.

'Have you checked the house?' the inspector asked me on one such occasion, his cap at the correct angle and his pockets bulging with official forms.

'Er, yes sir, it was negative.'

'Well, I'll go and check again, then.'

Sure enough, the child had slid off the bed and was peacefully sleeping in the gap by the wall.

To give the inspector his due, he didn't gloat; instead, with a mumbled, *"Do it properly next time"* he went to wait for his bus.

He was a genuine man whose leaving do was very well-attended, and attended by people who wanted to be there, for him, rather than just to use it as a get together, a free drink and to impress someone who could help them get on. His name was Dave Hart, better known as Daktari, as he had once been in the colonial police.

Another character was a sergeant, Mike McKewan.

On one occasion, I found myself dealing with the sudden death of a youngish man at home and the sergeant decided to visit me. There had been a cluster of sudden deaths, and undertakers were thin on the ground. I briefed him and we went into the house. He was fine at first and offered his condolences to the grieving widow and the children. There was a group of neighbours in there as well, all in dignified silence, apart from the wife's sobs. We stood quietly amongst them, caps in hand. Suddenly the radio burst into life.

'I said to him quietly, "The undertaker says that it will be a while before he gets to you sarge... All these sudden deaths, you know!"

He stood in the silent room with a look of frustration on his face. 'Why do all these people have to die at the same time?" he said, in exasperation. "It's a right pain."

Suddenly a look of awareness spread across his face. He didn't resist when I ushered him out of the house.

We were mainly unsupervised on the late shift and would only get the odd visit or two from the sergeant or inspector from Northwich. It was tempting – though strictly forbidden – for foot patrol officers to hop into a panda. One night I had joined Mike Vickers in his nice warm Vauxhall Viva for a ride around and a warm. As we drove up the High Street, we saw Sergeant Terry White coming the other way. Quick as a flash, I yanked the reclining seat handle and dropped like a stone into the horizontal position with my head on the back seat. I was feeling quite clever until the car started to slow down.

'Mike,' I said, panicking. 'What are you doing? Don't stop, you daft sod!'

'He's waving at me, I've got to.'

'Pretend you haven't seen him and drop us off around the corner!'

Too late, the car drew to a halt. The next minute, I was looking up at the frowning face of Sergeant White.

'Having a sleep, are we?' said Terry, as my seat slowly and embarrassingly came back to its proper position. I looked at Mike, who was looking straight ahead, hands firmly on the wheel trying to keep a straight face.

I nearly got caught again a few nights later. I was out with Mike, and the sergeant called up asking for my location for a visit. I pressed the 'speak' button on my radio at exactly the same time as Mike said, 'Tell him you're in Delamere Street.'

His thinking was that he could then nip back on to my 'patch' and drop me off there.

Unfortunately, Mike's 'Delamere Street' advice had come across clearly on the radio in the control room, and the occupants of every vehicle except ours burst out into uncontrollable laughter.

We were both interviewed at the police station at length, but we stuck to the story that I had been leaning into the car talking to Mike when the call came. Terry knew the truth, but he couldn't prove it.

Juveniles were dealt with differently then; sometimes it was for the best, sometimes not. On one occasion, I was nominated with another officer to convey a boy of thirteen down to a Juvenile Detention Centre in Staffordshire. He had been in court for the umpteenth time and had been given a spell in detention. This lad knew the score; he had been through the courts numerous times and was a recidivist.

'Get into the back of the car,' I said pulling the front seat forward for him.

'Yes, sir,' he said, and climbed in.

I dropped the seat and climbed into the front.

'Comfortable?' I said. It didn't hurt to make conversation and put him at ease.

'Yes, sir, very comfortable, sir.'

'What are you in for?' my partner asked.

'Burglary, sir, I broke into a garage, sir'.

'What did they give you?' I asked.

'Three months, sir. He gave me three months, sir.'

'Look,' I said. 'You don't have to keep saying "sir" all the time. What's your name?'

'William, sir, but they call me Billy, sir.'

'Stop it,' my partner interjected. 'Stop calling us "sir"!'

'Right, sir. Sorry, sir. I mean sorry!'

Finally, we got through to him, and for the rest of the journey we had quite a sensible conversation. He had nothing going for him: bad parents, in care, in detention, home to bad parents, back in care, back in detention. Soon enough, no doubt, detention would be replaced with prison. He was a very likeable lad, a loveable rogue I suppose. We even trusted him to behave when we stopped at a café for a snack, and he did. In giving him this respect and talking to him as a person and not a useless piece of rubbish, he responded. Eventually, we drove through the high gates of the detention centre and walked with him to the reception desk.

'Name?' said the stern prison officer behind the desk.

'Billy,' said the boy, at which he was picked up by the stern prison officer and thrown across the room bouncing off the wall. He got up, shook himself off and walked back to the desk resuming his place in front of it.

'Name?' asked the stern prison officer again as if nothing had happened.

'Billy, SIR!' shouted the boy, standing smartly at attention.

'Thank you, lad. You know the rules here. Let's start as we mean to go on, eh, there's a good lad!'

'Yes sir, sorry sir,' said Billy to the prison officer, looking guiltily at us. I gave him a sickly smile; in being nice to him, we had done him no favours. We had made him think that some adults could be pleasant.

As I progressed through my two years' probation, I took an active part in all aspects of police work. I also had the opportunity of leaving the police, as my brother Bill, an entertainment agent, had 'discovered' a band called Kindness playing at the Salter pub in Weaverham. He took over as their manager, changed their name to Smokey, and released an album – which was promptly banned from the air by the BBC, which believed it hinted at drug taking (given that it was entitled *Pass It Around* I suppose they had a point). The Motown singer Smokey Robinson then complained that he was known as 'Smokey', so the name was changed to 'Smokie,' and the band went on to become famous. They had more UK hits in the 1970s than The Rolling Stones, which creates a good pub quiz question, and were even more famous in Europe. Bill went on to manage other bands such as Blonde on Blonde, Hi Tension, and Chas and Dave, and went on to become wealthy and well-known in the pop world. I spent a lot of time off duty with him, going to gigs and meeting famous people, he offered me a job doing something lucrative. But I'd grown to love being in the police – too much to give it up.

Chapter Eight

Public Disorder & My CID Aidship

DURING THIS EARLY UNIFORM PERIOD, the demonstrations started in Holyhead by the farmers protesting at the importation of cheaper beef from Ireland. It became well-known for violent demonstrations, but I strongly suspected that most of the 'farmers' doing the protesting wouldn't know one end of a cow from the other. Unless farmers had taken en masse to wearing student-type clothes, silly beards, and long scarves, and waving the Socialist Worker placards. No, they were the usual rent-a-mob crowd as seen at virtually all high-profile demos for whatever reason – and who would eventually leave university and either become wealthy businessmen or Members of Parliament, where they could become dutifully incensed at the actions of the next generation

We were often called upon to police these protests. I remember my first time. The Cheshire Police contingent had travelled the ninety miles to Holyhead by bus, and we sat around for a while before we were put onto a train and taken down the line to a level-crossing which was blocked by a selection of cars and Land Rovers. I was quite new to this game, but I noticed that between getting on the train and getting off it the older officers had somehow lost the epaulettes which bore their numbers. Most had also removed their ties and tucked their trousers into their socks. Obviously, they expected some fun.

We all got off and stood in front of the crossing, protecting a heavy railway crane which had been brought up. A British Transport Police superintendent warned the demonstrators that if they did not remove the vehicles from the crossing they would be forcibly removed.

It's funny how things stick in your mind: as the superintendent was talking, one of the older officers in front of me was calmly having a piss on the ground! A 'farmer' who turned out to be a student from Aberystwyth University climbed on top of a Land Rover and shouted, in a rather high-pitched and squeaky voice, 'We've heard what the police have said comrades, and will move the vehicles!'

There was a grumble in the ranks of the downtrodden farmers and their young supporters.

'But not yet!'

Now it was the police's turn to grumble, until the superintendent shouted for us to be silent.

Then he gave the order to remove the Rent-a-Mob general and the vehicles.

I was in Sergeant White's serial, and we were nominated to move Mr Aberystwyth from his perch. I jumped onto the bonnet of the vehicle and joined him, and a look of fear suddenly crossed his face as he realised the war had started. Taking hold of him gently around the neck, I threw him off the roof of the Land Rover. As he hit the ground, I turned to see a television camera pointing first at me and then at him as he stood up to brush himself down. Luckily for me, the complaint culture had not yet set in.

The vehicles were all moved off the crossing in a very rough manner, farmers and students joining in to object as the nice paintwork was bumped and scraped. The Welsh farmers are, to this day, not happy about meat coming from Ireland.

This was also my first spell of 'special duty', which I soon realised meant big overtime payments. It wasn't always about rioting students, either. Oulton Park motor racing circuit is near to Winsford, and we regularly carried out traffic control for those entering or leaving. I remember spending one Saturday at a nearby crossroads, with the traffic lights turned off. After a day of constantly turning my neck at the sound of skidding tyres, I found blood on my collar where the skin had been rubbed away.

Of course, the mother of all such golden eggs was the miners' strike of the mid-1980s. It would be fair to say that Arthur Scargill was just as revered by the police as by his members, albeit for entirely different reasons. Unfortunately, I was on the CID by that time.

I was also on the CID when the race riots of the 1980s started, firstly in Liverpool, and then Moss Side. The police lost it in Liverpool, where 'appreciating both sides' and 'using empathy and understanding' was just becoming fashionable. Instead of just bashing them – as they did in Manchester, under Chief Constable James Anderton – the Liverpool cops were far more restrained. They had even donated a Transit van to the 'community' to use for social awareness reasons, old people taken to church, that sort of thing. Instead, it was painted black, armoured, and jokingly given the call sign by Liverpool policemen 'Rasta One', as it cruised the streets delivering ammunition to the rioters. For a while, anarchy reigned. One funny apocryphal story involves a PC who was found by a senior officer hiding in a doorway and told to get back to the front line.

'Sorry, sarge,' he is supposed to have replied.

'I'm a Chief Inspector!' said the other, indignantly.

'Bloody hell,' said the Bobby. 'I didn't think I'd run that far back!'

During my probation, I had spent time attached to the various specialist branches within the force. Prior to joining, I had liked the sound of the dog handler branch – walking around with a big dog to protect me – but this wore off after a week spent attached to a dog handler which I spent sitting in the front of a van all night with a smelly dog in the back barking all the time.

I remember one call when the handler and his dog went on a drugs raid. The handler got the householder in the bedroom and, using 'old-fashioned' police methods, got the man to tell him where the drugs were hidden. He then went downstairs and with his dog, stuck his head round the door of the room in which the team was searching.

'It's in that plant pot, lads,' he shouted.

Sure enough, in the plant pot was a bag of heroin. 'That's a clever dog,' said one of the searchers. 'He hasn't even been in here yet!'

The traffic department was ruled out as I didn't fancy just dealing with road traffic law and accidents.

That left the CID, which was a different matter. It appealed to my modus operandi, or being a bit of a cowboy, so I began my CID training, known throughout the country as 'aideship', in September 1976, just after finishing my two years' probation. I was based at Northwich police station, near my home in Winsford, under the wing of a tutor DC, John Atterbury, a tall and superbly fit man who spent all his available free time riding and racing pedal cycles around the country. John wasn't a 'seat of the pants' thief-taker, but he was dogged and good on paper and could be relied on to submit excellent files. He was never posted to the fraud squad, where he would have excelled and probably risen through the ranks, but instead promoted back to uniform as a sergeant, where he remained until he died aged fifty of a heart attack in 1998. He had just returned to his hotel in France where he was on a cycling holiday with his wife and his cycle racing team.

The Criminal Investigation Department of 1976 bore little resemblance to that of today. We had rules, but rightly or wrongly – and it largely depends on whether you want bad people off the streets or not – they were not followed as rigidly as they are now. Criminals knew their place, and they did not complain if their treatment was a little rough and their interviewing somewhat robust. It was part of the game, and there were very seldom any hard feelings. Even solicitors, told by their clients that they had been 'mildly assaulted' in the station, would suggest that it was put down to experience.

We liked to show our faces in the roughest pubs in the area – in those days before drink-driving was a major thing. We got some abuse, but the idea was to show that we were not frightened of them and there were no no-go areas, at least not in sunny Cheshire.

Prisoners were interrogated in order to extract the truth, and it was commonly believed that the end justified the means. This may have led to the strict rules of engagement we now have and the high-profile alleged miscarriages of justice. The implementation of the Police and Criminal Evidence Act (PACE) in 1984 transformed CID work, and police work in general. It has aided the criminal greatly and hampered the police for instance if they wanted a solicitor, we had to get them one. All the evidence had to be divulged to the defence, old fashioned seat of the pants detective work was out, and in my view has been to the detriment of society. The criminal element is a small one, but it is very busy. In the old days the police kicked its arse; now it must be treated in the same respectful way as the law-abiding society.

As a CID man, if you were good on paper but not the best thief-taker, you'd be alright. If you were a good thief taker and cut paperwork corners to get a result you were alright, too. If you were no good at either, you were back in a big hat.

There were the crime figures to consider. As now they were all-important and could make or break a detective chief inspector and the detective inspector. They were fiddled, thoroughly, and for a division to have detected crime figures of around 80%, as they often were, it took some fiddling. How? Let's say someone smashes Marks & Spencer's window in the early hours, causing £1,000-worth of damage. The crime report is intercepted by a detective, who marks it off as having been caused by a stone thrown up by a passing lorry. Accidental damage, no problem, no crime – and the fact that Marks & Spencer is in a pedestrian precinct is quietly forgotten by everyone, bar the uniformed officer who talks about bent CID bastards. M&S would get the paperwork for the insurance claim.

But the best crime figures scam involved prison visits. Some forces actually had an old detective doing nothing *but* prison visits. The rules of detection stated that prisoners could ask to see the police to 'clear their slates' in order that they could eventually come back into society with nothing hanging over them. Every so often, two detectives would visit the prison unannounced to see one of the scallywags whom they had dealt with. They would take with them the crime book, and a carrier bag full of chocolates and cigarettes to help matters along. As the prisoner munched his chocs and smoked his fags, the detectives would show him outstanding matters in the book to see which ones he wanted to claim. Technically, if he admitted a crime more serious than that for which he was inside it should be taken further, but it never was and most knew the score. So long as the prisoner didn't suddenly cough to a murder, he could admit anything he liked, and it would be marked as 'detected'. All he had to do was make a short statement stating that he would sign offences that he had committed in the crime book. So simple – and within reason it didn't matter how ludicrous the admission. I remember one Liverpool shoplifter, who only had form for shoplifting, putting his name to the theft of pedigree pigs from Bunbury in central Cheshire. The piece de resistance? If their signature was amenable to forgery, further scribbles could be added in by the more unscrupulous officers on their way home, while parked up in a lay-by.

These should not be confused, by the way, with 'TICs' (offences taken into consideration at court, before sentencing). This was another method of clearing up crime, but they tended to be genuine since it was in front of a magistrate or judge. Prison visits were the preferred option all round.

My detective chief inspector at the time was Roy 'Dixie' Dean, who went on to be a detective superintendent and – as so many coppers seem to – died very soon after retirement. Dixie, a superb detective, had been heavily involved in the Moors murders inquiry – I think he found the bloodstains on the floorboards – and was a nice chap. He had a habit of punctuating his sentences with a liberal use of the word 'there'; the detective chief superintendent had a similar habit, though his verbal tic was 'the question is'. When they did a joint briefing, it could be difficult to keep a straight face, what with Dixie firing out 'there' every three words, and his boss repeatedly saying 'the question is'. One officer ticked off about twenty 'the question is-es' before he was caught. 'I know what you're doing Ball,' snapped the chief super. 'Bloody stop it.'

It was a relatively unexciting period, during which time we mounted such huge ops as that to clear the homosexuals from a local picnic area just off the A556. Numerous complaints had been received from children and parents about the activities of men in a prefabricated toilet in the car park. There was a 'Ladies' on one side and a 'Gents' on the other, and they were joined in the middle by a corridor containing cleaning gear, the chains for the cisterns, and two peeping detectives. As soon as anything started, we would run round and open both locked doors simultaneously with a screwdriver. The occupants were often too busy to notice our presence, until a few discreet coughs and perhaps a comment on the weather disturbed them and they would stop and be arrested.

None of us were happy with the duty, and the upset and embarrassment it was causing to the offenders, but children being propositioned, and suggestive notes being left to read by anyone just could not go on. It was sad somehow to see a grown man walking furtively into a toilet cubicle, with a bag containing sandwiches and a flask, probably made up by his unsuspecting wife for him to take fishing or trainspotting. It takes all sorts, too; during that operation we caught a welder, an artificial inseminator, a Crown Court clerk, and assorted businessmen. I remember one man whose daughter was getting married at the weekend; another was a Church of Wales vicar who joined me when I was using the urinal for a legitimate call of nature. He stood next to me, winking, and looking down, and when I had finished, I gave him a good bollocking and asked him what his flock would think if they saw what he did between sermons. He departed very sheepishly.

Another early job saw me bollocking a bishop. We were having a lot of thefts from churches at the time, and the cleaner at a church in the market town of Middlewich had seen a scallywag leaving with the brass candlesticks and alerted the parish priest, who was also the Catholic Auxiliary Bishop of Shrewsbury. The bishop bravely went after the thief, caught him and brought him back to the presbytery. A cup of tea was produced, and they had a cosy chat, during which the chap explained that he was unable to feed his children and was going to be thrown out of his house because his wife didn't understand him. He said he had never done anything like this before, was at the end of his tether and didn't know where to turn. I was filling up myself until the point where his lordship explained how he had given the fellow some money and sent him on his way *before* calling us. I pointed out that this chap had been bang at it, and if we could only have got hold of him, we might have prevented similar thefts in the future. The bishop was humbled, not least because the felon went straight to Chester Cathedral and stole the candlesticks from there.

Chapter Nine

In plain clothes waiting for a CID post.

I completed my aideship, and the two-week CID Aides course, and was due to return to uniform, but a vacancy arose for a plain clothes officer, and I got it. I covered the whole division, mainly dealing with criminal damage, sex offences, and the like, reporting to what was then called the 'Women and Children's Department'. In those days, policewomen tended to work in this specialist department dealing mainly – as you'd expect from the name – with women and children.

While working in plain clothes, I met a legendary Merseyside detective sergeant by the name of Bill Boden, who had been seconded to the Regional Crime Squad at Runcorn. There had been a particularly nasty rape at Widnes, and I was sent to work on the inquiry and teamed up with Boden. We received some information about the whereabouts of the suspect and set off to take up our position. We parked up in Bill's black Austin Princess on one side of the large sports field attached to the Wade Deacon School and waited for him to show up.

Bill was a lunatic – the story was told that he once petrol-bombed a gangster's house after the gangster left a pig's head on his doorstep – and a man of appetites. He chain-smoked Capstan Full Strength cigarettes (which he eventually gave up, on doctor's advice – though he replaced them with Hamlet cigars, not on doctor's advice), and could put away twenty pints of Guinness at a sitting. I do not exaggerate; you won't be surprised to hear that he died relatively early. By late morning, and with no sign of our rapist, Bill decided that we would leave the plot and seek sustenance. He drove to a local watering hole where he was well-known, and I had a pint and Bill had a couple of pints of Guinness. We then went back on plot, but Bill was soon bored again so we went – for some reason – to a spice factory, where we were both given some packets of spice by the owner. On the way back, we stopped at a club Bill knew, and he had another three pints of Guinness (to my one of bitter). Back on plot, where he immediately called in to ask if we could leave to deal with a call of nature. Our first legal one, and we were given permission. Back to another pub for Bill to have three pints of Guinness to my half of bitter, and then back on plot.

Shortly after our return on this final occasion, the suspect was seen walking on the other side of the sports field.

'We'll take it,' said Bill into his radio, and the heavy Princess started to hurtle across the sports field at breakneck speed. Too late we both spotted the sunken running track, with a drop of four foot, as it loomed into view at about 60mph.

'Oh shit!' said Bill, and with that we sailed off the edge.

Incredibly, the car bounced back up in a shower of cinders and on we sped on towards the terrified suspect, who turned out not to be the suspect after all, but a chap walking his dog.

We drove slowly back to our plot.

This style of working was all new to me, though I can't say I didn't enjoy it. This was the policing later immortalised by Gene Hunt in *Life on Mars* when the CID kicked arse and got results. When you didn't have to call scumbags 'sir', and when if a bloke looked like a criminal, talked like a criminal, and acted like a criminal, he almost certainly *was* a criminal, and coming to that conclusion didn't make you judgmental, it made you a good detective.

After the rape inquiry, it was back to ordinary plain-clothes work for a while. I managed to have allocated to me a Vauxhall Viva ex-panda car, which made life easier as I covered the whole division, which included Winsford and all the surrounding villages.

By now I had investigated a few indecency offences – 'flashers and the like – and I became quite good at it. I nabbed one prolific Northwich 'flasher' who even 'flashed' his own barrister in her chambers at the Crown Court. Flashers invoke humour, but they cause upset and distress to the women who they flash at, and some go on to commit much more serious crimes. Mostly, though, they are harmless and sad individuals.

I came on duty one morning to be told that a woman who had in the past provided me with information had, during the night, disturbed a man in her back garden. Her story was that she had approached this man and been stabbed in the stomach. Knowing the area, and that neither she nor her husband were innocents, I was not totally taken in. Other officers had been, however, and had spent the night at her hospital bedside while dogs searched the gardens for evidence. The detective sergeant was a chap I didn't really see eye-to-eye with; I thought he was a nasty piece of work, which in fact he was – he was rough with prisoners, even rougher than I was.

I collared him that morning. 'That stabbed woman, sarge,' I said. 'Bit iffy, don't you think?'

'No, I don't,' he said, pompously. 'An offence has been committed and the CID is looking into it, so you can go off and chase your flashers.'

'Well, I know her,' I said. 'Do you mind if I give her a visit?'

'Do what you like,' he said, dismissively. 'I've got better things to do, like set up an incident room. It's what detectives do, you know!'

I visited her, and it took me ten minutes to extract from her the fact that she had slashed her own stomach with a razor blade because her husband had intimated that he was leaving her, and she wanted him to stay.

'Where's the razor blade, you soft sod?' I said, handing her a cup of tea I'd brought.

'In next-door's garden,' she said. 'I threw it there.'

'Why didn't you tell them last night you daft bugger?'

'That big bloke, the DS,' she sniffed. 'He was a prick. I thought, *no, why should I, I'll stick to my story*, and I sodded him off. What will happen, Paul? I won't get in trouble, will I?'

'I can't say,' I said. Honesty is always the best policy. 'It's up to him and, as you say, he's a twat. So, I wouldn't hold my breath.'

I went up to her house and saw her husband, told him what she had done and looked over next door's fence. There, lying on a paving stone in the lawn, was a half razor blade smeared with blood. I called a uniformed PC and asked him to get the scenes of crime officer back to take possession of it. I didn't bother with the DS; I went over his head to the DI and told him what had happened. He was no fan of the DS either and couldn't wait to have a pop at him.

The woman was later reported for wasting police time, but it never went to court.

In 1978 I was involved in the to-date unsuccessful investigation into the murder of an old farmer called Leslie Guntrip in a picturesque cottage near Winsford. He had been repeatedly struck about the head with a blunt instrument, although the duty inspector had apparently initially decided that he had fallen and hit his head on the metal fire surround. The story goes that the body was then to be taken to the hospital mortuary, but on the arrival of the CID at the house, several bloodstained dents were noticed in the low ceiling immediately above where his head had been, suggesting an implement repeatedly raised and brought down on the unfortunate man. The inquiry lasted for two months, and at the start of it I was notified that I had successfully passed the examination to sergeant. I was then qualified to sit the inspector's exam, but with the ongoing investigation with long hours worked, I was unable to study, and I failed the exam. I did not, to my great regret, attempt it again, to date no one was arrested for the Guntrip murder.

Chapter Ten

Back to uniform and tutoring a future leader.

In 1979, with no vacancies in the CID, I returned to uniform at Winsford as a tutor constable. One of my successes was Derek Barnett, a very pleasant ex-steelworker with an innocent manner and a subtle sense of humour. As a forgetful probationer, Derek's favourite trick was to leave at least one item in all cars that we stopped: gloves, helmet, torch or note book, it didn't matter. What was awkward was the subsequent chase and stopping again of the motorist who had just been well and truly told off. 'Excuse me, can I have my gloves/helmet/ torch/note book back?' takes away some of the dignity and impact of the occasion. I wrote in Derek's 'Probationer's Handbook' that he would make superintendent within twenty years. I was nearly right: he finished up as a chief superintendent, President of the National Police Superintendents' Association, and an OBE.

On one of the first night duties with Derek, we went out on patrol. After we had purchased our usual chips and curry sauce, we headed for a quiet car park to eat it. As we drove in, I saw a man with a ginger beard sat in a Mk 1 Vauxhall Viva obviously eating his chips. My suspicions were aroused when, on spotting us, he started his engine and screamed out of the car park virtually on two wheels. I gave chase, and a high-speed pursuit ensued. I lost sight of him as he rounded a bend in the road that led to a narrow bridge and dirt track leading to the village of Moulton. As we rounded the bend, the first thing I saw were his headlights pointing at each other. He had struck another car in the rear, the driver of which was an elderly gent with his wife and friends who were sneaking back to Moulton the back way to avoid the police and their new-fangled breathalysers.

'You look after them,' I said to Derek, 'and I'll go and see how that bloke is.'

I walked over to the Vauxhall and looked into the driver's side. The driver was slumped over the steering wheel, but all I could see in the dim light was a bare white back with a black bra strap across it.

Strange. I'd not spotted a woman in the car. And how on earth had he got out?

He hadn't, of course. I pulled the body upright and told it to get out of the car. It was the same man with the beard; he was fifty-odd and wearing a small, black, mini-dress, and high heels. He staggered from the vehicle, chips spilling everywhere, drawing gasps from the old people in the other car. They were quiet Cheshire folk and not used to being rammed from behind by bearded men in a sexy frock; surely that sort of thing only happened in London? After obtaining their details, they were allowed to sneak off home and the chap in the black bra was reported for reckless driving.

I also gave Derek a lesson in how to deal with people threatening to commit suicide. One time a man was on the roof of a house threatening to jump off, and his family and the neighbours were in the garden pleading with him to come down.

'What are you going to do?' I called up.

'I'm going to fucking top meself,' he shouted back.

I questioned him a bit further until, I'm afraid to say, I became bored. I'm not good at pandering to people who obviously just want attention.

I cupped my hands and yelled up, 'Well, we've another job to go to, so when you jump, try not to land on anyone. We'll be back to pick the bits up shortly.'

At that we left, and on returning half an hour later he was in the house having a can of beer.

One of the two permanent Winsford sergeants was Wilf Batchelor, a typical old style Cheshire sergeant. One day we were called as two large cygnets had flown into a power cable and been killed. Locals were distraught at the sight of the two lovely swans lying in the field. Wilf had the answer.

'Shove them in the boot of the car lad,' he said, out of the corner of his mouth. 'Nicer than turkey, they are. Why should the Queen be the only one to enjoy 'em?' although she owns them, and doesn't eat them...

The birds were reverently picked up and placed in the rear of the police car, amid promises of a nice burial in the police station garden, and we drove off. That night Mrs Wilf prepared them for the freezer.

The other permanent Winsford sergeant was a tall officer called Tony Goode, and younger than Wilf. He was out with me one day and we were having a brew at one of the factories on the industrial estate when the radio buzzed into life.

'Oh, God, help me!' wailed a voice. 'This hasn't happened, what am I to do?' It was one of the probationers, John Lawrence (in this instance, I've changed his name). 'Someone come and help me to sort this out! Oh God, no! Oh, please say this hasn't happened!'

We managed to get his location, and as he continued to send panicky messages about many deaths and carnage I set off for the narrow, pre-dual carriageway Winsford High Street.

An incident within an incident then occurred; as we drove down a hill, a car pulled out of a side road and bumped into a cyclist. As we shot past, the cyclist rolled gently over the roof and down over the boot onto the road. We didn't have time to stop, and I never heard any more about it.

When we arrived at the scene of John's panic, we were indeed faced with a scene of apparent carnage. A double-decker bus had its top deck almost severed, and a man was trapped between a wall and a girder on a lorry. Glass from the bus windows covered the area like glistening snow. John's black gloves lay forlornly on the footpath amongst the debris, and children sat around looking dazed.

The lorry, which had a long iron girder sticking over its cab roof, had needed to back into a narrow entry. John was in the vicinity and the driver asked him for help.

'No problem,' said John, who had only just been allowed out alone and was seizing a good opportunity to help the public. 'I'll stop the traffic, and you back in. Don't worry, I'll direct the traffic around the girder.'

Wasn't this the reason he had joined the police in the first place?

Quite simple and straightforward, just an ordinary day in the life of a young probationary police constable. John held up the traffic for the lorry to back in. Then, with the girder sticking out into the road, he directed the cars around it... until the driver of a double-decker bus full of schoolgirls drove into it and peeled the top of the bus off like a sardine tin.

But that wasn't all! At the same time, the lorry driver had climbed on to the back of his wagon and was between the girder and the wall. When it connected with the bus, it squashed him.

The scene was quite spectacular, and I could understand John's panic – it looked like he had caused the deaths of one lorry driver, about two dozen schoolgirls, and his own career.

As it happened, the girls had all ducked, and the driver was only bruised; the main injury was to John's pride, and he had a lot of writing to do. He recovered to enjoy many successful years on the job, mainly in the CID.

Violence is a fact of life in the police. One officer I worked with quite often was a powerfully built man, but a gentle giant, Big Kev Taylor, called Big as there were two Kevs and the other one was small. – working with him, I was always getting attacked.

On the first occasion, we were called to the local rough pub on the poorest of the council estates as two men refused to leave. As we arrived, they were standing outside the pub being abusive; most of the customers were taking their side and a riot was brewing. 'Let's lock them up and chuck them in the car,' I said. 'If we hang around here much longer, they'll all kick off.'

'We shouldn't really put them both in one car,' he replied, quite rightly.

'Can't be helped,' I said, taking hold of one of them. 'It's either that or a riot!'

We locked them up without handcuffs, and fortunately they came quietly. I then had to drive to Northwich, some seven miles away. This was a recipe for disaster and would never happen nowadays. A mile into the journey, one of them spoke up.

'You're a pair of twats,' he said. 'Just because you wear a uniform you think you're it. You don't frighten me. I could take you anytime.'

We had heard it all before and ignored it. But I couldn't ignore what came next. I was driving up a slight hill towards a bend, a single decker bus coming towards me, and all was well with the world. The next thing I knew, the gobby prisoner had grabbed me around my neck with both hands and pulled me across the back of the driving seat.

I managed to keep the tips of my fingers on the steering wheel, and – trying frantically to reach the brakes – aimed the car at where I hoped the roadside hedge would be, and not the front of the bus. I then passed out due to the pressure on my neck.

I came to moments later with the feeling of pins and needles in my face. The bus had vanished, and the car was rolling gently back down the slope with both my partner and the other prisoner struggling to subdue my assailant (the other prisoner I assume thinking that, in trying to kill us all, his mate had gone a bit too far). Between the three of us, the fat idiot was eventually restrained and cuffed, and we carried on with our journey. I had two things in my mind. The first was that point in training where they had told us to think money if we were assaulted, as it eased the pain; the second was to wonder why I hadn't smacked the stupid bastard as hard as I would normally have done. To this day I don't know why.

At the police station, we accepted the expected bollocking for not handcuffing them at the scene – even though it would probably have caused a riot and meant us getting battered. Often, in the police, you just can't win.

A week or two later, back on patrol with my strapping friend, we went to a terraced house to arrest a local youth on suspicion of theft. He was in the back yard, fixing his bike.

'I'd like you to come with us,' I said. 'We need to talk to you about something.'

The lad acquiesced, but I heard a shout. It was the suspect's father, who was a paraplegic and confined to bed in the downstairs back room.

'You're not taking him anywhere,' his father yelled through the open window, pulling himself up in his bed with a handrail to get a better look at what was going on.

'Sorry mate,' I said, 'but he's locked up.'

I took hold of the lad, who came quietly, and I'd just reached the panda car when I was suddenly hit from behind and spread-eagled face down on the bonnet. The next minute a fist came round and struck me in the side of my face.

Momentarily stunned, I grabbed out at the prisoner – except that it wasn't him. His father, by some superhuman effort, had commando-crawled out of the window and down the path, and somehow launched himself onto my back. He gradually pulled me to the floor, and I continued to take a shellacking – my partner proving quite useless – until his wife came out and told him to stop.

He lay there, clinging to my back, panting.

'Get off me,' I yelped.

'I can't!' he cried. 'Me legs have locked, and they're tangled up with yours.'

He was right, too. It took his wife some time to free him, and I was finally able to stand up and put the son in the back of the car.

'Are you going to lock him up too?' asked Kev, nodding at the old man.

'Oh, yes,' I replied. 'And no-one will take the piss when I push his wheelchair into the charge room and say that he has assaulted me, will they? Let's just put him back to bed.'

Football matches were another place you expect to get beaten up. Our nearest team of note was Northwich Victoria, and on the 14th December 1976, they drew Peterborough at home in the FA Cup. For small teams they had big hooligan firms, and our job was to stand between the two opposing groups on the terrace. I was with another PC, called Dave Large, and it was getting a bit heated, with plenty of verbal exchanges, when suddenly Dave shouted out in pain. I looked at him and saw that a dart had hit him squarely in the cheek, or gum and was sticking out as it would on a dartboard. He instinctively put his hand up to pull it out and I grabbed his arm and stopped him.

'You've just got a small prick,' I said jokingly. 'Let's make sure lots of people see it.'

I led him from the ground, making sure we walked past as many photographers as possible, and that they got a good look at him.

Sure enough, some rather spectacular pictures appeared in the papers the next day, and Dave got a decent bit of compo.

Uniformed policing offers all human life, spread out like a canvas to be viewed, and sometimes enjoyed. This is especially so on our rougher council estates. It can get annoying, too, visiting these modern-day slums. In my early days, police pay was terrible – one of our kids had free school meals after I was means-tested. I used to find it frustrating to leave home to go on a winter nightshift, my family in a house that was cold because we couldn't afford to turn on the central heating and go to an early hour's domestic call to a council house where no-one worked, or had ever worked, and it was too hot to breathe inside. Minus six outside, and the heat is emanating from the front door, the complainant standing there in a T-shirt. My thoughts would turn bitterly to my own children, huddled in overcoats behind iced-up windows.

On one night duty, I went with Bob Woby, the sergeant, to a sudden death on one of the estates. It was winter, and it had been snowing. The family were rough and anti-police, and their newborn baby had died – it was a cot death. The unpleasant job of checking a dead body for suspicious signs falls to the reporting officer – me. To do this I needed to be left alone with the baby, so the sergeant ushered the family out of the room and shut the door. As I turned the baby over, its stomach contents went over my leather gloves. There was nothing suspicious and I went outside. Bob was talking to the father. I went over to a wall, quite a way off, to clean my gloves and scooped some snow from the top of the wall. At this, the father looked over at me and shouted, 'My fucking baby's dead, and that bastard's making snowballs!' There was no real answer to that.

Now and again, however, it does not pay to be anti-police. Another unpleasant job is the delivering of sudden death messages. It's a duty that is carried out with the highest degree of tact, diplomacy and understanding, for obvious reasons. On one occasion, I had to go and tell a woman that her father had died suddenly. On arrival at the terraced council house, I found a party in full swing, and it was very noisy. I hammered on the door and after quite a while, the upstairs window opened, and a woman looked out.

'What the fuck do you want?' she shouted.

'Are you Linda Smith?' (made up name) I shouted back.

'Yeah. And?'

'Can you come down, please?' I said. 'I need to talk to you.'

'No fucking chance,' she shouted. 'I've got far more important things to do than speak to you bastards. If you haven't got a warrant, fuck off.'

What would any caring and considerate person do when faced with such a situation? I certainly drew on all my reserves of empathy, consideration and understanding, before cupping my hands to my mouth and answering her. 'Your dad's dead. Goodbye!' The party noise emanating from the house suddenly went silent.

On another evening, we got a call from the ambulance service asking for some assistance. We went to a dirty house in which we knew a middle-aged woman lived with her family in surroundings of absolute squalor. In the porch we met the ambulancemen.

'What's up lads?' I asked.

'We've had a report that someone is injured inside, and he won't come out.'

'Why don't you go in and get him?' I said, fanning away the smell and heat that emanated from the open door.

'Bugger off! Have you seen the state of the house?'

So, we went in, squelching across a black carpet that had once been red. We found the woman of the house, in all her twenty-eight stone of unwashed glory, lying on a couch in the kitchen. Filthy curtains covered the brown windows and the arms of her settee shone darkly in the dim light. One of her offspring, aged about sixteen, sat by her, looking very sorry for himself.

'What's up, Jean?' I said, trying not to gag.

'Wayne's fallen downstairs,' she spat. 'Them bastards won't come in and I know he's hurt himself because he was sick in the stew.' She indicated a pan which was simmering away amongst the fat and filth on the stove. It was then my turn to run out and refuse to come back.

Wayne eventually came out and was dealt with. Whether the family ate the stew, I never found out. Neither did I want to.

Travellers have a shocking reputation for general nuisance, and many of them do seem to enjoy camping on private land and destroying it with their vehicles and the rubbish they leave. Some undoubtedly rip off the public – especially older people – with shoddy work and overpricing. Today the police have various laws which can assist in controlling them; back in 1979, it could take weeks for the ponderous wheels of justice to move them on, and in the meantime the area of the camp often became a disease-filled tip that would cost thousands of pounds to clear after they left.

We were called out by a farmer whose field had been taken over. He was not happy as he knew he'd have to pay for the court hearing to get them evicted and would then be faced with a disgraceful mess – not to mention, he also needed to use the field.

'What do you want to do with it?' I asked innocently.

'Well, when the grass grows, I'll turn it into silage.'

'I assume you'll have to spray it with a muck spreader' I said. 'You know, to make the grass grow?'

'Well, yes,' he said, looking at me quizzically. Then enlightenment dawned on his weather-beaten old face.

'Well, it's your field!' I said.

And off he went to get his muck spreader, while I went to meet the travellers, who assured me that they had only stopped to give the children a bite to eat. Sure, they would leave straight away.

'No problem,' I said. 'But you might want to keep the caravan windows shut!'

Just then, the tractor lumbered into view, its noxious trailer dripping brown stuff onto the road. They were hitching up and leaving in minutes.

As luck would have it, a week or so later I was called to a traveller's wagon that had broken down and was causing a big traffic jam. I spoke to the driver, and he told me that he only wanted a small part for the engine. I knew this could be purchased on the other side of town, and this chap seemed okay.

'Get in the car, mate,' I said, 'I'll take you to get the part.'

This was purely to expedite the removal of the truck and did not reflect my love of travellers.

Off we went, and I stopped at a parts shop. He was back in a jiffy with the crucial item.

'I'm very grateful to you, sir,' he said, in a strong Irish brogue. 'I'll have to give you something for your trouble.'

He took £10 from a bulging wallet.

'No, that's alright,' I said. 'I'm not allowed to accept anything.'

'Oh, just ten pounds, sir. Surely I can give you that?'

'No, it's alright.'

'I'm very grateful to you. Just ten pounds.'

'No, thank you.'

'Well, I'll put it in this here glove compartment,' he said, opening it up and putting the note inside.

'Nice day we're having, isn't it?' I said. 'Oh, here's your wagon. Goodbye.'

Well, I couldn't force him to take it out of the glove compartment, could I? And I certainly couldn't leave it in there!

Other than getting that tenner forced upon me, I've never accepted money for anything regarding my duties. Actually, I tell a lie. When we attended a sudden death in those days, it was the practice for the undertaker to attend alone and for a policeman to assist him with the body. Getting a stiff body down flights of sometimes very tight stairs was difficult and undignified and, as paramedics will confirm, people who are feeling ill always go upstairs to lie down. For his trouble, a PC would be handed a one-pound note by the undertaker as he left. Just a token of gratitude, and a big saving for the undertaker compared with paying an assistant the going rate. This continued with all sides happy, until a Sunday paper found out about it and exposed it as one of the most corrupt practices since Watergate.

This was the beginning of the end for all the big corruption scandals, such as getting a free cup of tea at motorway services, or a cheap bacon butty at a café.

Not that newspaper reporters would ever do anything dodgy!

Chapter Eleven

CID at Last & the Ways and Means Act

IN APRIL 1981, I BECAME a detective constable at Winsford, and found my vocation. We had a good office, small by the standard of others, but very busy.

The aim of a good detective is to obtain the services of good informants and it was in that that I excelled. Informants were usually recruited in the charge room after they had been arrested for something; you tapped them up and put them to work passing on information.

There was friendly rivalry in the office to clear up crime and the ways of going about it were quite fluid.

There was a definite CID culture, but even its days were numbered.

Most nights, the drink-driving laws not being quite as rigidly enforced as they are today, the officers on duty would go out and spend the evening boozing. This was literally our job – it was expected that we would get round the pubs on our patch, and 'meet people'. It was where the villains were, after all. In the rougher pubs there'd be plenty of banter and some abuse; all of the 'baddies' knew who we were, and some were not happy about the sometimes-rough treatment they had received in the police station.

One night, we found ourselves in the Wheatsheaf, near the Mount Pleasant estate.

'There's a fucking smell in here tonight,' sneered a voice. We were used to this, but we did not accept it (unless the abuser was unusually large). 'Somebody must have let some pigs in.'

The voice turned out to belong to a teenager full of lager and bravado and surrounded by his smirking mates. I walked over to him.

There are various tried and tested ways of dealing with this sort of thing. One is to say something like, 'Hello Dave,

I didn't see you there. You've not phoned me for a while, I thought you'd moved.' Or 'I suppose I've paid for that ale, have I? You've had enough informant money lately; you should be able to treat your mates!' Always good for a laugh when their friends suddenly look at them in a different light and the bravado disappears. Or you can be more direct, as I was on this occasion.

'I'm sorry, mate,' I said, in the dignified and official police officer manner as taught in the training centre. 'But if you're referring to us, I'll fucking bounce you.'

He looked away sheepishly as his mates giggled at him. We'd finished our drinks anyway, so we left. As we got outside, our abuser came flying through the door backwards and landed in the road.

'You're barred,' said the landlord who had helped him on his way. 'Sorry about that lads. He's an idiot.'

That support was not always forthcoming, for many reasons. It's very hard being a landlord in a rough pub, and the Wheatsheaf was a classic example.

Often what happens is that first the brewery puts in a quiet, unassuming landlord who is severely abused by the local thugs and must leave. He is replaced by a hard nut who gives as good as he gets, and that usually ends up with him being arrested for going too far. So, another nice landlord is parachuted in, but this time members of the hardest local families are employed in the pub. So, peace reigns for a while; but the pub stops making any money, as the tills are constantly down. It's a difficult balancing act, and the right man must be like gold dust.

Sometimes the info came from an informant with no evidence to back it up, just a rumour. Let's say you have a lad in for a burglary at an old lady's house, based on intelligence from a reliable informer. It could be wrong; it could be right.

The idea was to behave as if you knew far more than you really did. There's no point in asking, 'Did you do it, Billy?'

Billy simply says, 'No.'

'Are you sure?'

'Er, yes.'

Straight away, he knows you're fishing, and either clams up or has time to think of a story to keep you on the back foot. The job's lost and you might as well walk away, as happens now under PACE.

That's not to say we don't go fishing – we do. It's just that the first few seconds are crucial.

I'd start with, 'Right, Billy. Been a bit daft, haven't you?'

'What you talking about?'

'You know full well what I'm talking about. Don't take me for a fool, lad. Now give, or I'll have to do something about it!'

Now he's on the back foot, wondering what you know. Depending on the inbred daftness of the suspect, an admission to something else may come.

'Do you mean the shoplifting?'

'No.'

'The motorbike?'

Let it run until he has finished admitting lesser crimes.

'No. I'm getting bored now, Billy. I'm talking about the house. You know, the one on the Barratt estate. That's the one that we've got the best evidence on. I'm not saying that is the only one, I'm saying that it's the one we can prove.'

Hopefully – and in a percentage of cases it happened – the reply would be something like, 'Come on, Paul, what will I get if I admit that?'

Foot in the door. He will also have to provide some real evidence – like the property that he took or where it went, just to make sure he really did do the job – but the rest is easy, and he'll clear his books. Under the modern rules, detectives have their hands tied. You certainly wouldn't get away with stuff like that if a solicitor was involved. But can someone please tell me what's wrong with it? I'm not talking about beating confessions out of innocent men, that's wholly wrong. You're engaging in a battle of wills to try and put away a man who – you believe, based on reliable information – stole an old lady's most treasured possessions.

Of course, informants get things wrong, and it may be that Billy really didn't do it. When it becomes obvious that he doesn't know what you are talking about, you put your arm around his shoulder.

'Got to try, mate, haven't I?' you say. 'What if it was *your* grandma's house? You'd want me to pull all the stops out, wouldn't you?'

People who rob old ladies take it very personally if it happens to one of their loved ones. So yes, he takes your point, and suddenly your friends. You take him for a drink, and now you have a new informant. And so, it goes.

This is simplistic, but it gives you a picture. In the bad old days, detectives were crafty, and far more crimes were detected. Nowadays, officers rarely even *speak* to suspects without a truckload of evidence. The problem is, in most cases there never *is* a truckload of evidence. Yes, we also fiddled the crime figures – but instead of crime reports in the DI's drawer waiting to be slipped in somewhere or taken on a prison visit, the fiddling is official.

A good ploy we often introduced was to use humour to lighten interviews.

On one occasion there was a burglary through the roof of a shop. As usual, we had nothing to go on other than a reliable informant.

'Aye up, Billy,' I said, when I came across my man walking down the street. 'We need a chat in our office, I think. Come on.'

He climbed into the back of the Mini, grumbling that he was innocent and hadn't done nuffink.

At the office, I sat him at a desk and told him that he was in the shit.

'What do you mean?' he said, eyes wide. 'I've done fuck all!'

'You're not in the shit with us, mate,' I said. 'Calm down. We're here to help you.'

'What're you talking about?'

'You did that shop through the roof last night.'

'No, I…'

'Hang on, hang on. Let me finish. You never got permission to do it, and another couple of lads were due to do it and you got in their way.'

'What the fuck you talking about?'

'You never cleared it with Eddy,' I said, giving a well-known local gangster's name. 'Any grafting in Winsford now has to be cleared by him to save getting in each other's way. You didn't clear it with him, and if we don't deal with you, he will.'

'Honest?'

'Yeah. If we, do you, you'll have had your punishment and the slates clean. If we *don't,* you're on for a good slap!'

This kind of thing happened a lot. Sure enough, Billy had the job off me.

Petty criminals are not, in the main, endowed with much brainpower – otherwise they wouldn't be petty criminals. For instance, the following year the same Billy drove his tatty old black mini van along the pedestrian precinct in the early hours and backed it through the plate glass window of the Radio Rentals TV shop. He loaded a few televisions into the back and drove away. The detective who attended found a nice piece of evidence lying amongst the broken glass – the vehicle's licence plate. Half an hour later he found Billy at home, watching one of the stolen tellies and celebrating the job with a can of beer.

These days their solicitors take a far more active role, and the culprits are a bit brighter. If you leave your number plate outside the shop you've just ram-raided, you're probably still in trouble, but apart from cases like that the public often don't get much satisfaction.

Of course, solicitors will say they perform a good service. Do they?

One of the bouncers at a local disco saw a youth arguing with his heavily pregnant girlfriend. It got progressively worse until he kicked out at her. The girl left the club and sat down on the kerb crying, and the doorman went to comfort her. The boyfriend came out, saw what was going on, and ran at them both in an aggressive manner. As he reached them, the bouncer simply put out a plate-sized fist, and it connected with the boyfriend's chin. His head hit the kerb with a crunch, and he was instantly unconscious with a fractured skull. He remained in a coma for several weeks.

It was down to me to interview the bouncer. Depending on the answers he gave, irrespective of the rights and wrongs, he had committed an offence. I did what I was to do on many more occasions and dealt with it in what I felt was a humane and sensible way – a course of action that is getting harder and harder to follow as our actions are ever more circumscribed. I asked him what had happened. I deduced from what he said that if he gave the wrong answers, he could be in a lot of trouble, mainly in view of the serious injury sustained to the boyfriend. This would have to go to the Crown Court and what he said now would have long-lasting implications and be extremely important. I also knew that if he called for a solicitor prior to interview, the advice would possibly be to make no replies: although this may enable the solicitor to line his pockets, it would not help his client.

'Will you trust me?' I asked him.

'Yes,' he replied.

'Then you will have to set your stall out now. Pleading not guilty will not help you but highlighting the facts and admitting to those will.'

I wrote out his statement and arranged for him to see a solicitor afterwards. He went to the Crown Court and, as expected, walked free. This course of common-sense action worked for many people that I dealt with, an option that has been taken away by the hordes of naïve and not so naïve do-gooders.

Solicitors and the CID have a love-hate relationship, but it's not as simple as it seems. Weirdly, the investigating officers can be a suspect's best friend and his lawyer his worst enemy. Many's the time I've known suspects be advised by their solicitors to plead not guilty despite a wealth of evidence against them. The offender is then well and truly hammered in court, whereas if he'd admitted it and apologised, he'd have been dealt with more leniently. Solicitors often seemed to me to be more interested in the money that they received from the Legal Aid Board or the suspect than the outcome of the case.

On the other hand, I got paid at the end of the month and that was that. There was no financial incentive to me to twist things. I locked up offenders, simple as that. If there was good reason, I'd help them if I could. If they were recidivists, screw them.

Like when the uniform section nicked a group of five travelling Liverpool shoplifters. They'd mistimed the arrest and the stolen items had been dumped. Still, all five were put into the cells at Northwich and, being scallywags, they knew their rights.

They immediately began hammering on the cell doors.

'You're going to have to let us go, you thick woollyback bastards,' yelled one, using a popular term of abuse used for us simple country folk. 'You've got no fucking evidence!'

And indeed, they were eventually released. They left the station in high spirits, shouting abuse and ridiculing the officers in rich Scouse accents.

A short while later, one of my uniformed colleagues came to see me.

'You know those shits that we've just let go?' he said. 'On the way out of town, they stopped at a second-hand shop and one of them took an old set of kitchen scales from outside. Totally pointless – it was only worth about two quid. The shopkeeper says they were laughing at him and taking the piss.'

'Leave it with me,' I said, with mischievous seeds of vengeance maturing inside me. I was aware that one of them had to report to Admiral Street police station in Liverpool that night to sign on as a condition of bail on a different matter. I contacted the CID there, and I have to say they were most helpful. As the given lad came into the police station, a detective entered the porch and arrested him.

After a short while, three of his mates came in to find out where he was. They, too, were arrested. The officers then went to their car, and in the boot, they found the scales. An escort was sent to look for the fifth youth, who had been dropped off somewhere, and the other four were brought over to Northwich.

What I would normally have done in similar circumstances – had I been feeling less vindictive – would be to have put them in a cell together to decide who was going to admit the theft. When one did, he would be interviewed, and the others allowed to leave.

But this time I thought I would be a thick woollyback. (It's probably worth pointing out here that I am actually a Liverpudlian myself – but I can pass for a woollyback if required.)

'It's getting a bit late now, lads,' I said in my daftest country accent, as they were being booked in by the sergeant. 'I'll interview you tomorrow and I want you all to tell me the truth. If you don't, I really will get annoyed.'

There were derisive smirks all round.

If that wasn't throwing down the gauntlet, nothing was. They were bedded down for the night, and I circulated the other one as wanted.

The following day, I interviewed them one at a time and asked them if they had stolen the scales. I even cautioned them, which shows the lengths I was going to in order to prove that I *was* a thick woollyback bastard.

Most policemen in the 1970s didn't bother with the caution. Many didn't even know the words.

As anticipated, all my Scousers denied the theft, with varying degrees of sarcasm.

They were returned to their cells. A short while later, the fifth man was arrested. He came in with outrageous claims that he had been 'verballed' on a breathalyser. The Liverpool police had stopped him in his car at 9.30 that morning, and his account of what had transpired was as follows.

Policeman: 'Morning, Billy.' (They all seem to be called Billy.) 'Been drinking, have you?'

Billy: 'No.'

Policeman: 'Well, we want a breath test from you.'

Billy: 'OK, no problem.'

Policeman: 'Fine if that's how you want it. You're under arrest for refusing to provide a specimen of breath!'

At the police station, the sergeant said, 'I'll give you a second opportunity to give a breath test.'

Billy: 'I've already said I would.'

Sergeant: 'Alright, refuse if you want. Will you give me a blood or urine sample?'

Billy: 'Yes!'

Sergeant: 'Alright, don't then. But you'll be charged with refusing and will get a ban. Oh, and by the way… you're wanted in Cheshire for theft.'

According to the charge sheet, which would be put before the magistrates on his return to Liverpool, Billy's reply to this was, 'The magistrate's wife's a whore.'

Poor Billy. Those awful Merseyside policemen!

On his arrival at Northwich, Billy was placed in a cell. I secreted myself in the cell passage with a notepad and recorded what was said between the gang – and they actually did say this.

Billy: 'Who's having the fucking job?'

Voice 1: 'No-one. That jack's thick.' (A 'jack' is slang for a detective.)

Voice 2: 'Get X to give the shopkeeper a fiver and he'll drop the charges, like last time.' (X being a well-known Liverpool solicitor.)

The shouting went on for a while and I duly wrote down what they said. All were later charged with the theft of a cheap set of scales and bailed. I submitted my notes as an exhibit in the case.

As expected, they came to court pleading not guilty. They were particularly cocky as they stood smirking in the box, but my contemporaneous notes nailed them, and they each received three months in prison.

As I passed them later on the way to the prison van, they were at pains to point out that their solicitor had given me a hard time in the witness box.

'Maybe so, lads,' I said. 'But I'm happy enough. Where you off, anyway? I'm going for a pint myself!'

Woollybacks five, clever Scouse bucks, nil.

Travelling Liverpool criminals were the bane of Cheshire and other neighbouring counties. I remember talking to some lads from the Liverpool Stolen Vehicle Squad.

Places like Northwich are like the stones round an overflowing bin,' he said, sagely. 'The rubbish lands there when the bin's full.'

How right he was.

Situated on the Division was Delamere Forest, an area popular with walkers and picnickers who would leave their cars at the roadside and in the car parks. These areas were popular with Scouse scum who entered the cars looking for chequebooks, cards, and money, which they later sold on in the pubs back home.

With another DC, I arrested a team who were seen acting suspiciously, and interviewed them at Northwich. Nothing was found on them, and at first nothing was admitted. But I knew they were at it, and, under a little pressure, they agreed to admit all they had done in exchange for us not objecting to bail.

I took down a comprehensive statement, outlining all the cars that they could remember breaking into, and jogging their memories on one or two others in the crime record book. The agreement was that, after court, and when they had been bailed, they would sign a form containing a list of other offences to be taken into consideration. This was normal practice, especially if they were not likely to get prison, although signing the form merely confirmed their receipt of it. Then, although the judge or magistrate would take them into consideration and might order some compensation to be paid, they could not be punished for the offences admitted.

We charged them with one or two specimen charges and bedded them down for the night. I then approached the detective inspector, Derek Lidster, who was at the time quite new.

'These lads have cleared the books, boss,' I said. 'I've promised them we won't object to bail. That's okay, is it?'

Normally, CID supervision honoured deals like this – without them, the offences would not be cleared up, so it was a small price to pay – so I expected the usual nod of agreement.

'They're Scousers aren't they,' said Derek. 'Fuck them. We're not doing them any favours. Object. Have we got evidence?'

'Well, yes, they've made statements.'

This was unusual and good work on our part.

'Fuck 'em, then. Make 'em stew. Bastards, coming over here thieving. I'm not having it.'

He wouldn't budge and so we had to object to bail.

After court, I met the offenders whilst they were on their way out – the magistrates usually gave bail, despite strongly-worded objections by the prosecution on our behalf. They called me a double-crossing bastard and various other names, along with instructions as to where I could shove the T.I.C forms.

There was only one thing left to do: they had admitted the offences in writing, so I prepared about seventeen charges and they were hit with those on their next appearance at court.

At the Crown Court they pleaded not guilty. Among other things, their barrister said to me, 'Is it not true, officer, that you punched my client in the stomach and hit him over the back of the head?'

Addressing the judge, I replied innocently, 'This, Your Honour, is an allegation frequently made by Liverpool barristers which is totally without foundation.'

Fortunately, the judge believed me.

They were duly found guilty and sentenced to periods in prison, which was not a bad result, given that they were never caught with anything, just acting suspiciously. The salt in their wounds came when the judge formally commended me and my fellow DC for our efforts.

I have to say, I prided myself on being an up-front detective, and I didn't like working this way. They'd been okay with us, and I would rather not have opposed bail. It was quite likely that I'd end up having to deal with them again, and this would make it harder. But Derek was right, too. These toe rags were coming to Cheshire, smashing car windows, and destroying innocent peoples' days out.

This kind of policing was about the Ways and Means our way of saying that if there were ways to get evidence, criminals were fair game. A large red Lincoln Continental town car had been seen frequently driving about on the streets of Winsford. Cars like this were rare, especially in our neck of the woods, and everyone had noticed it. One day, an informant told me that the car had been set on fire in Liverpool as an insurance job. He told me who had done the burning.

I checked and, sure enough, the car had been reported stolen and been recovered burnt out in Liverpool – not in itself an unnatural occurrence, but it all tied in with my informant's story.

If I got the owner in, he would deny it.

If I got the burner in, *he* would deny it, too.

In comes the Ways and Means Act.

I brought in the alleged offender. 'I'm afraid you're in a bit of shit, son,' I told him.

'What do you mean?' he said.

'Mr Smith's downstairs in the cells,' I said. 'He's made a full admission regarding his red Lincoln.'

I was employing a little poetic licence here, in the sense that Smith wasn't in the cells and had made no such admission.

'What's he said?' asked the offender, his mind working overtime trying to think of a way out.

'You know what he's said. Don't fuck about. You torched it for him for the insurance.'

I waited for an answer and duly got the one I was after.

'Come on, he's been having money problems, I only did him a favour.'

After formally interviewing the burner, Smith could then be arrested, and that admission put to him. As a result, he admitted the offence straight away.

That way of working would be frowned upon today – but why? Those offences *had* been committed, by *those* offenders, and no innocents had suffered. The word would go out that Cheshire CID were hot on the tail of anyone involved in insurance jobs.

Such crime is serious and widespread. Fraudulent 'thefts', 'burglaries' and 'robberies' cost insurance companies millions of pounds each year. If you pay insurance, you are footing the bill in increased premiums. But the allegations are very hard to disprove, and their investigation is a delicate matter; in many cases I fear the police no longer have the time, or resources, to get involved beyond dishing out a crime number.

I developed an excellent little trick based on my 'thick woollyback' persona – a persona too easily assumed; some might say! A report would come in of – say – some silver taken in a burglary. I'd go into the house, sit down, and take the details of the 'offence' before shaking hands and leaving with assurances that we would do our best to recover the property and catch the thief. Ten minutes later, I would 'remember' that I had left my briefcase at the side of the chair out of sight and return to humbly ask for it back. Then I would leave a second time – but then I would rewind the mini tape recorder concealed within. If it was an insurance job, nine times out of ten I'd hear the words, 'Do you think he fell for it?' This was of no evidential use, but it often helped me to obtain a retraction of the claim.

*

There are serious aspects to police work, though, and it can be quite sad. There was always a duty detective on lates, usually working from 6pm to 2am, and any crime in that period was down to him to investigate.

One night I was called to a big house which had been converted into flats, where a man's body had been found hanging from a rope. I found the uniformed duty inspector in attendance; he informed me that he had already called the on-call DI because the death was suspicious.

I suppose it was, at first sight: the chap had clearly died from hanging, but he also had his hands tied behind his back and his feet tied together.

I swung the body to one side and walked past it into the living room. There I found a comprehensive suicide note, which included the fact that he was going to tie his own hands and feet to stop himself from bottling out. From other material around the place, it was clearly in the dead man's handwriting, and I confirmed that all the doors had been locked with no sign of a struggle. It was a simple suicide but in those pre-mobile phone days I couldn't cancel the DI and he turned up and agreed with my findings. The job was then handed back to the uniform section to deal with it and prepare the coroner's report.

I was happy to have made that call myself. If you're getting paid as a detective, you have on occasions to make decisions without shouting for second opinions.

Like the Warrington DS who I was to work with later who attended the scene of a death in a flat that was covered in blood. The victim's neck was slashed and there was blood everywhere. He soon deduced that if you slash your jugular vein blood squirts a long way and as the man flailed about in his death throes, blood was squirting out of his neck as it would from a hose. The DS made the decision that it was a suicide, and it was the correct one. Many others would have called in additional officers for confirmation, to cover their backsides.

These things are not nice to see, and the police – as do the Navy and other services – use black humour as a way of coping. I've seen many dead bodies, and there's rarely any dignity. A woman found dead in her kitchen on her hands and knees attracted some undignified comments. One elderly lady collapsed on the floor, and as she went down her false teeth came out. When I lifted her head up, I saw that they had embedded themselves in her eye socket. Not funny, but strange. I had to insist that the paramedic left them there for further investigation.

Earlier in my career I attended at a house where smoke was seen coming from a bedroom window. It was about 4am and I booted in the front door – later, I was told off by the fire brigade, as my actions could have fanned the flames. It was irrelevant as it happened; the old lady living there had fallen asleep smoking, and her bed had become a smouldering BBQ. By the time I arrived, the bed had collapsed into the floorboards and she had cooked from the waist down. The top part of her body was intact, and a young policewoman and I followed the undertaker to the hospital. Our job there was to remove her valuables and keep them safe. She had a ring on her finger, and I told the WPC to remove it. As she pulled at the ring, the skin came away under it like a finger bandage. The policewoman went green, and I had to take over. Think of that the next time you're complaining about police brutality, or a road closure. This is the kind of stuff young officers are doing day in, day out.

I attended many post mortems during my career. It was the detective's job to list anything the pathologist felt may be relevant, and this could include many different body parts. One of the most unpleasant bits is bottling the stomach contents – effectively, vomit. The smell is always atrocious, and I once pointed out to a pathologist that this was the worst part of the job for me.

'I've been doing this for twenty-seven years,' he said. 'It's the worst bit for me, too.'

Some of these pathologists could be very strange people. One, known as Benstead the Beast, would turn up in an MGB sports car, wearing a loud suit and a big flowery dickey-bow. He was certainly good at his job, but it must have affected him over the years. He'd ask the mortuary attendant to get him some sandwiches; when they arrived, he'd simply pull his hands out of the body, wipe them on his apron and tuck in.

Another pathologist removed the vagina of a woman, opened it up and spread it on the table.

'Look at that,' he said. 'Men take nine months to get out of it and the rest of their lives trying to get back in!'

Chapter Twelve

When You Don't Know What to Do, Go for a Drink!

IN THE LATE 1970s, the senior CID posts at Northwich had been taken by what came to be known as The Taffia. As in The Mafia, but they came from Wales.

As it happened, DCI George Jones was Welsh, but he and his DS Dave Finlay brought a new meaning to the word ruthless. The job had to be done and everyone had to get results, and he didn't care who he told or how he told them. Runcorn came under the wing of Northwich, and the head man there – DI Geoff Underhill – was not one of the Taffia, but an easy going and likeable officer.

One morning, we were in the office at Winsford when Geoff Underhill, the on-call DI, visited. We had a brew; a chat and he checked and signed our pocket books.

I was on till midnight, and due in at 10am the next day. But the phone rang at home very early. It was Alan, the morning man.

'You'll have to come in, Paul,' he said. 'There's a body in Sandiway.'

'I'll be right there, is it suspicious?'

'Well, they're trying to get hold of DI Underhill,' he said, 'so it must be a bit iffy. The body's been set on fire.'

Not long after, I walked into the police station to find Alan ready to leave. 'They still can't raise Mr Underhill,' he said. 'I wonder if he IS the body.'

He laughed at his own black joke.

We arrived at the scene – it was a country area just off the A56, not far from Underhill's home.

The duty uniformed inspector was present. He had stood astride the body and had been the one who asked for the DI to attend.

Now he was ashen faced. 'Hello lads,' he said, sombrely. 'It looks like this is Underhill.'

The body was black, its features and clothes burned away, and suddenly we felt guilty about the jokes we had been making on the way there.

It turned out that he'd been depressed for some time and had gone from the house when his wife awoke. A petrol can from beside the body was identified by her as having come from their garage. The Detective Inspector had committed suicide by pouring petrol over himself and setting it alight.

There was naturally enormous sympathy for his family, and for the man. But Alan and I had to deal with the body, and we had little sympathy for the way that he'd done it. He was a policeman, he knew his colleagues would have to deal with the after-effects, and that his family would have to identify him. That said, his mind must have been in turmoil for him to do something like that.

A new DI took over at Runcorn, Jock Marshall – he and the DI at Northwich disliked each other with a vengeance. Jock was a devious and ruthless Scotsman who was not averse to ducking and diving, a la *The Sweeney*, in the way portrayed on screen by ruthless city detectives of the period. He left the police for medical reasons during an investigation into his actions. The Northwich DCI George Jones went on to run the force CID and he did it well as the detective chief superintendent. Like a lot of CID senior supervisors of that era, if you worked hard and got results, you could be forgiven many faults and expect support when your actions backfired for genuine reasons. You must be good at paperwork and in the interview scenario. If you could not fit these criteria, you were out.

Every so often, a Crime Conference was held within the division when current crime trends could be discussed. It was in the days before the obsession with anything that could be construed as racist, however tenuous. During one of these conferences, Jock Marshall, said that he was fed up with Liverpool criminals coming into Cheshire and thieving. In future, he said, if any Scousers come here, they are to be arrested, because they must be 'up to something'.

As I said earlier, I am a Liverpudlian – I was born in the city centre, lived there and started school just off Scotland Road. I love the place but am under no illusions as to the level of criminality that it both suffers and exports.

That night, I was on duty with another DC called Mark Tunstall, when we had a phone call from a pub on the outskirts of the town. It was an off-duty PC, who told us that there was a group of Scousers in, playing on the fruit machine and drinking half pints of beer. This was suspicious: the words 'half pints of beer' and 'Scousers' did not usually appear in the same sentence. He told us that he would watch them leave and give us their direction and registration number. He duly did this and said they were coming towards the town. We had them stopped as they entered the town centre.

'Where are you from lads?'

'Liverpool, we're going to visit my aunty.'

They were asked the usual questions about the car. The driver said it belonged to his aunt and told us correctly what was in the boot. Everything seemed in order. Mindful of the detective inspector's words earlier in the day, we decided we would have to do something, so we arrested them on a very weak suspicion of stealing the car. The car was taken to the yard, and they were taken to the cells.

'What do we do now?' asked Mark.

'Fuck it, let's go to the pub and think about it,' I replied. It was getting near to closing time, so we had just got time to have a drink. Over the pint, it was decided that Mark would go and have a word with them, and I would have a good look at the car.

Under the carpets throughout the car, I found a fortune in ten pence pieces with some wrapped in electrical tape. In those days you could put a fifty pence piece in fruit machines and get five ten pence pieces out, with which to play. The trick was to put together five ten pence pieces and wrap electrical tape around the edge to a certain thickness, then cut each ten pence off in the same way as cutting slices off a Swiss roll cake. For each doctored ten pence put into the machine they got five ten pence pieces back as change – the machine mistook the taped coins for a fifty pence piece. These lads had been following the Liverpool football team around the country, hitting every fruit machine en route and emptying it of ten pence pieces. Jock was right, at least that time anyway. They were charged and pleaded guilty.

Following on from this mention of DI Jock Marshall and policing in what was then the very early 1980s, there is another incident of note that could have gone horribly wrong.

Jock had friends who ran a pub locally and there had been a spate of robberies in public houses where the managers or licensees had been tied and gagged. Unfortunately, Jock's friends received this treatment, and a team was arrested in Liverpool for similar offences. Jock suspected that they were responsible and had them brought to Northwich. He then ordered myself and DC Alan Brocklehurst, my mate, to interview them 'properly' – he did put emphasis on the word properly.

We went over and started the interviews and after a few hours of intensive and rather robust chatting we both formed the opinion that he had got it wrong, and they weren't responsible. Returning to Jock's office we told him of our findings. His reply was in keeping with his way of working and went something like this:

'Bollocks, I thought I could trust you to get a cough, that big bastard had an earring in when he was brought in, is it still in his ear?'

'Yes boss.'

'Well go and interview them properly then.'

We left to follow orders and have another go, during our interview with 'the big bastard' he lost it and screamed at the top of his voice launching himself at us. In police speak we restrained him!

Jock had to let it go, I for one did not intend to get any heavier with these lads and we were both quite happy that they were innocent, at least of that one job.

I thought that was the end of the matter and life continued as normal.

Chapter Thirteen

My first real complaint

NOW IN THOSE DAYS a complaint against the police was usually investigated firstly by a superintendent and (you've guessed it) the 'big bastard' made a formal complaint about his treatment; even in those quite ruthless days this did not happen often, certainly not like today when the police are fair game and daren't step out of line. I wasn't aware that Alan Brocklehurst had been summonsed to Northwich for an interview by Superintendent Robinson, known in the division as 'Dickey Mint'. He was a good boss who did not suffer fools and like me had the good name of the force at the back of his mind.

Brocky returned a bit ashen faced.

'It's your turn now, a bit iffy this.'

We didn't say much more, and I headed for Northwich and my interview.

'Hello Paul, do you know why I've called you here?'

'Yes sir.'

'Did you interview some Scousers a while ago over pub robberies?'

'Yes sir.'

'Who with?'

'DC Brocklehurst.'

'Did one of them scream during the interview.'

'Yes sir.'

He looked up startled, 'Do you know what you're saying?'

'Yes sir, it's in my pocket book.'

'In your pocket book, thank God for that, hand it over.'

I did as I was told and he read that during the interview, one of the suspects lost control of himself, screamed, and attacked us, no offences were disclosed, and the interview continued.

'The superintendent smiled, picked up the phone and told Alan Brocklehurst to 'get his arse back over here'. (At which I suspect Alan wished for brown trousers).

'This Paul is what I wanted to see, I hate these toe rags getting one over on us and this was one bad bastard. Do you know the scenes of crime officer who was up here at the time, two floors away, provided a statement saying that he heard the scream, and it was the worst scream that he had heard in 25 years' police service?'

I mentally and cynically thanked John Dobbie for his attention to detail. John was straight as a die and had even refused to recover a house brick from inside a car because he suspected, quite wrongly, that it had been planted there. He was a lovely man who sadly died shortly after retirement.

I don't think Alan had made a pocket book entry but mine saved any further trouble and we heard no more.

Sticking with the ruthless Jock Marshall, politics played a large part in the internal machinations of the CID in the 1970s and 1980s. Personalities were all important; careers were made and destroyed during public house conversations between senior and not so senior officers. Prior to this, the CID office would have the same detectives for many years. Now, room had to be made for the up-and-coming young thief takers who were prepared to go out and lock up by whatever means necessary, fair, or foul. The saying 'you are only as good as your last job' became important. If you had not had a 'last job' for a while, or a perceived while, you would have to go, by whatever devious method.

In the Winsford CID office, there was an old detective constable who had been there for many years. He plodded along and dealt with jobs that came in and this just was not good enough for the new brooms. It was accepted that each night, the DC who was first on the following morning would, if he so wished, take home one of the CID Mini cars. It was not officially sanctioned but was an accepted practice.

'Where is the yellow Mini?'

The question was directed by phone to the night detective from detective inspector Jock Marshall. He knew very well where it was because, with the detective sergeant, he had just seen it up the old DC's drive.

'I don't know boss,' came the reply.

'Go and check the yard,' he was instructed and ten minutes later he phoned back.

'No, it's not there boss,' he said, truthfully this time.

DC Bill Baker (not his real name) was sitting at home; he had just enjoyed a full supper and was making the most of this period of relaxation. He was in his carpet slippers and watching the television. Bill only had a few years left to serve and most of his career had been spent in the CID. He was an old time 'Jack' and could look forward to finishing his time, getting a nice, commuted sum and a monthly pension. Life had been good to him.

'There's someone at the door love,' called his wife.

As Bill opened the door, he was faced with the detective inspector and the sergeant, the offending mustard coloured Mini sitting in his drive behind them.

'Hello Bill, what's that car doing in your drive?' asked Jock pointing at the CID car.

'I'm on at seven in the morning boss, you know the score.'

'I'm afraid I don't know the score, Bill. I want you to submit a report tomorrow asking to leave the CID, or I will lock you up for taking this car without consent, do you understand me?' Turning round, they walked down the drive leaving Bill standing at the door making mouth movements like a fish.

The following day a report duly went in, and Bill was returned to uniform 'at his own request' and made the office man at Winsford. He had a modicum of revenge when he exchanged the old desk in the front office for the new one that he had occupied on the CID, thereby leaving the CID office with four new grey desks and a tatty old blue-topped one.

This politicking was mainly amongst the senior officers, although getting on and staying on the CID was a position to be fought for and protected. Even as a PC without having done any CID training, if it was your intention to apply, you had to show your aptitude by whatever means necessary. Submitting undetected crimes was not one of those means and the submitter would be remembered if his application came through! If as a PC he had made no effort to water down the crime reports that he put in, it would not go well for his application There were sycophants both in the CID and those hoping to be in it.

There was still plenty of humour though, especially of the black variety. One day we got a call to say that a body had been seen at the edge of Winsford Flash – a big lake surrounded by countryside. We managed to get to the body by walking through a field and down a steep bank. The man had been fishing and it looked like he had had a heart attack and collapsed head first into the water. How on earth were we to get his body, which was in the sitting position, completely stiff with rigor mortis, to somewhere a hearse could park? As an off-duty officer with the Winsford Sea Cadets I had an idea. I would go and get the motorboat!

When I got back with it, they had managed to sit the man on the bank. We eventually got him into the boat and thought that it would be a good idea to sit him in the stern. We then set off back to the Marina, attracting little attention from the sailing boats that we passed. The only suspicious thing was that the unfortunate man sitting in the stern was sitting bolt upright and looking at the sky all the time. When we reached the Marina, there were more people about and we had to cover him up before the hearse arrived. All in a day's work.

One of the last stories of 1980s detective work involves an armed robbery at a garage; the lad was caught nearby, and the DS asked me to interview him properly – we hear that comment quite often don't we? I took him into an office and thought immediately that he looked quite young.

Interviewing juveniles was and is a complete pain. Most are as streetwise as any adult – some more so than most – but before interviewing them an adult is needed, a solicitor will be called and with no good evidence the job is going nowhere. He had nothing on him to tie him in with the job, but I gave him a full comprehensive interview ensuring that I never mentioned his age. He was completely streetwise, and I built up a good rapport with him. He admitted the job. He had used an air pistol and the money had been hidden. I then took from him a statement under caution and when completing it his date of birth had to be written down.

'Is that really your date of birth Billy?'

'Yeah.'

'But you're only fifteen!'

'Yerra know.'

'You should have had an adult with you, why didn't you tell me?'

'Me mam would never come out anyway.'

'Well, I will have to interview you again with an adult here, but you know now that I'm straight and I'll look after you, hang on here a minute.'

'That lad was only fifteen,' I told the DS, 'and I've interviewed and coughed him!'

With a twinkle in his eye, he told me to take him to Northwich, picking up the stolen and hidden money on the way and re-interview him with an adult present. In view of his family's total disinterest in him it would have to be a social worker.

I did as I was instructed and took him over to Northwich. A social worker arrived with a rolled-up Guardian sticking out of her handbag. It was pointed out to me in a well spoken and high-pitched voice that I shouldn't have interviewed him, and that interview was null and void. I agreed but pointed out that he looked older; I also pointed out that the offence was armed robbery, and it was quite serious! We re-started the interview with her sitting beside the lad. I cautioned him.

'Now Billy, because I wasn't aware that you were under age, I must interview you again in the presence of this lady, do you understand?'

'Yeah.'

The social worker said haughtily. 'You don't have to admit anything Billy, you do know that don't you and you don't have to reply to anything. I'm here to look after your rights?'

'Fucking shut up you stupid bag, I've already told Paul the truth and that's it. Don't know what the fuck you have to be here for anyway, you dick!'

Well, I couldn't have said it better myself, I did tell you he was a streetwise little sod! He re-signed his statement and she counter signed it and I wrote up the file in a way that he would be dealt with as leniently as possible.

CID work then really did require quick thinking at times, on another occasion, again with a juvenile, I was the night CID man, and a youth was brought in by one of the uniform lads. He was suspected of burglary. I had a few words with him and left him for the uniform lad to deal with. That, as far as I was concerned, was the end of the matter, no statements, no involvement. Three months later I was in my wellies working in the garden when a panda car pulled up outside.

'They've adjourned the court for you and want you to attend.' I had no cases due; surely, I had not forgotten a case? Still in my wellies I climbed into the car and went to Northwich magistrates. As I entered the court, I looked at the defendant and did not recognise him. I saw the reporting officer sitting there and it started to dawn on me what this was about, and it was iffy to say the least. I walked to the witness box leaving a load of my garden on the carpet and I stood and took the oath; the solicitor was Quentin Querrelle, a very well-known local solicitor and one who I had the greatest respect for.

'Officer, do you remember on such an evening interviewing my client?' He indicated the smirking youth.

I addressed the magistrates, 'I do sir, I remember speaking with him.'

Quentin's eyes opened wide; he was expecting a total denial. 'You do remember officer; can I remind you…?'

I interrupted him and turned to the magistrates, 'May I address your worships as I may be able to assist here.' The chairman nodded. 'Your worships, I am a detective, and it is my job to detect crime. To this end I can speak with anyone that I want to. Naturally I am fully aware of the Judges' Rules that dictate that juveniles must be accompanied by an adult when interviewed. I spoke with this lad, but naturally the conversation was about offences that he may be able to assist me with, but only offences committed by others, not himself.'

I looked back at Quentin, and he said, 'No further questions!' and sat down.

Outside he caught up with me and just said 'bastard!'

I smiled and asked him what he expected me to say.

I used to meet 'Q' on occasions in a pub that we both used, and we would chat about old times. After I retired in 2002, he asked me what I was doing with myself, and I told him that I was doing some freelancing and writing a book about the war.

'Fiction or non-fiction?' he asked.

'Fiction,' I replied.

'You always were good at that,' he said with a sarcastic smile. Quentin was one of the few solicitors who were made Crown Court recorders. He sat as a judge at Chester and Mold Crown Courts. Sadly, he passed away some time later.

Chapter Fourteen

Fun and games on the Junior CID course

AFTER SERVING FOR A WHILE AS A DETECTIVE CONSTABLE and before qualifying for further progression in the CID or other specialist duties such as the Regional Crime Squad, it was necessary to attend the Junior Detective Training Course. This was a national course with various venues, Wakefield, Liverpool, Preston, and London to name but a few, and once you were nominated it was potluck where you ended up.

I went in 1983 to the Lancashire Police Training Centre at Hutton Hall, Preston. This was a ten-week course, and it was known as 'the best course you will ever go on'. In Cheshire, you went as a serving detective and unless you really were useless, it did not affect your career. In North Wales for instance, you attended as a police constable, and it was a condition of your getting in the top 50% for progression to the CID.

The course curriculum covered pure crime with obscure subjects like criminal bankruptcy, blackmail, and child destruction. It was hard; each Monday there was an exam.

That sums up the academic side of the course, but equally important, no, that's wrong, more important, was the social side. Detectives are by nature of the work they do, party animals. If they do not display a propensity for wine, women, and song, then it is, or rather was, deemed a drawback that would result in someone asking them if they would not rather wear big boots and sort out the sheep and traffic.

The course lived up to all expectations. Prior to attending, it was usual for prospective students to open a secret bank account in order to hide their monthly informant and expenses allowance from their wives or partners in order to fund the course. On my course, there was a Royal

Air Force police sergeant who in the first week managed to spend £400. In 1983, that was a lot!

Sadly, this course was the downfall of many marriages because of the temptations open to the students. Class would start at 9am and finish at 5pm. After tea the sportier students would then visit the gym for an hour, the rest of us would have a lie down. This would be followed by two hours' study and then out on the town. The Squires nightclub in Preston was the favourite and actually had CID groupies. A dance floor conversation involving new students would go something like:

Her: 'What do you do for a living?'

Him: 'I'm an airline pilot.'

Her: 'Is that right, what are you doing this week? Hang on, week one, the Theft Act.'

Him: 'OK, it's a fair cop, any chance of a shag?'

The delights of Blackpool were reasonably close by and one of the lads, I will call him Steve, went there one night, and met the woman of his dreams. Despite being married and living five miles from the training school, he managed to stay over every night and even had to do 'gate duty' for a full weekend! What amazed him most was that this woman, the one in the Blackpool nightclub in the mini dress and glitter, said that she was a virgin. He had taken her back to her granny's bed and breakfast and then into a room.

They sat kissing, him allowing this 'virgin' admission to sink into his drink-addled brain. When the petting got a little warm, he called a halt.

'No, no, I won't be the one to deflower you, I respect you too much.' They carried on kissing and once again it got a little heated.

'Stop it,' he slurred, 'this is going too far.'

She sat back from him and looked him in the eye, the light reflected from the glitter on her face as she answered him.

'Steve, it is you I want, I have waited for this day all my life. Make love to me Steve, I want you, I want you now!' So, he did.

The following Monday we all met in the dining room after the weekend break and Steve pulled me to one side.

'I've got a dose, I can't think where I got it, but I think I've got a dose of VD.'

'I know where you've got it from you daft sod – the virgin, that's where you've got it from.' He continued to insist that he couldn't have got it from her, as she was a virgin.

'What woman of twenty-two, up to her eyes in glitter in a Blackpool nightclub, letting you shag her on the first night, would still be a virgin?' But he wouldn't have it.

I went with him for moral support that evening when he went to the clinic at the local hospital to have the diagnosis confirmed.

In the large hospital grounds, we couldn't find the clinic and came upon some old cleaning ladies having a fag on the steps. He discreetly asked them where the Genito-Urinary Clinic was.

'You mean the Pox clinic luv,' a rather plump one in a smock replied loudly, 'it's just over there.' She spoke in the diplomatic way unique to middle aged plump women cleaners smoking fags.

'Got a dose 'ave you luv, he's got a dose Mavis, dirty get; you should 'ave kept it in yer trousers luv, could 'ave ad me, I wouldn't 'ave given yer a dose.'

We walked away with the manic cackling echoing around the car park and drawing the attention of everyone present to Steve's embarrassment. The diagnosis was made, he had caught NSU or Non-Specific Urethritis. To the class it was VD, a dose of pox!

'What am I going to do?' he asked as we sat at dinner, 'the doctor told me I couldn't have sex for about eight weeks, what can I tell the wife?'

'Bloody hell Steve, you haven't given it to your missus?' said one concerned classmate, an evil look of glee on his face.

'No, I stayed the weekend with the virgin didn't I, lucky that, I've still got to tell her that I can't shag her for eight weeks though and on top of that I've got to get the virgin to see the doctor – shit, I wish I'd been born without a knob!'

A competition was then held amongst the class to find an excuse for Steve to give to his wife. The winner was the lad who remembered that a policewoman in London had been bitten on the back by a prisoner and had caught syphilis from him as a result. That was the way to go and elaborate plans were put in motion. During the week one of the class phoned his wife, stated that he was the station sergeant from Blackpool and asked to speak to Steve who obviously was not there. On the Friday, Steve phoned home and told her that he would be late, as he had to go to the hospital for a check up, he had assisted the police in Blackpool to arrest someone and the prisoner had bitten him.

'Oh, yes,' she had replied innocently, 'the sergeant from there phoned up asking for you the other day!'

Two hours later he went home to be met with a barrage of love and tenderness, he was a hero; of course, she understood that he had caught something from the prisoner that he had bravely arrested. It didn't matter that he couldn't make love to her. He was her brave little soldier, and she would look after him and care for him.

By Sunday he felt so guilty and such a rat that he told her the truth. On Sunday night he returned to his room at Hutton and was shortly after divorced. I believe that he has now married his 'virgin'.

Other impromptu excuses had to be thought up to excuse other fornicators; one lad wore a surgical collar for four weeks when he went home as he had received a minor neck injury in the gym. This prevented his wife seeing the necklace of love bites that he had acquired from one of the groupies who no doubt knew exactly what she was doing.

Another had to explain to his one-nighter that he had borrowed his brother's car with the baby seat in the back. He had been declaring his undying love as the front seat reclined romantically into it when parked in a lay-by.

As mentioned, every Monday there was an exam and although most of the students were happy with the social side, there were swots too, boring farts whose one aim was to progress in the service and get out of the CID on promotion as soon as possible. The worst of them would go around the rooms at night shouting for the noise to be kept down because they were studying. Sometimes this noise couldn't be helped, especially if it came from a woman in the throes of ecstasy. One even got on the stage before one exam and told everyone – to a barrage of cat calls – that he thought we were not professional. The next Monday he was not at the exam. He had gone into Preston one lunch break, presumably to stock up on prayer books and lemonade. He had stood too near the road and had been struck by the wing mirror of a heavy truck, fracturing his collar bone. He would not be back. There was an undignified cheer from the room.

Humour and 'wind-ups' were my thing. The CID office at Winsford was on the second floor of the old police station and was entered by going up a tight staircase from the hall below. The staircase had a bend in it and came up directly in front of the toilet, which was on the landing between the two offices. Now the toilet bowl itself was set back about six feet from the door in a long narrow cubicle. The door could be opened quickly from the outside with a screwdriver. One morning DS Hood went in to enjoy a relaxing read of the paper whilst attending to the call of nature. On duty in the uniform section was a woman sergeant, a very well built, humourless woman with the demeanour of an old-fashioned matron. I phoned downstairs to speak to her.

'Hello Sarge, the DS would like you to come up and see him as soon as possible.'

She agreed and I nipped out and opened the toilet door to see the DS in all of his glory sitting on the pan reading the paper. Because it was an all-male office, when people did childish things like this, you just ignored it and carried on reading; you could not reach the door to shut it anyway without getting up. This time it was different: the DS was faced with the severe persona of the 'matron' standing on the stairs in front of him, her face level with the toilet bowl, and there was nothing much that he could do about it.

'So, this is why you want me to come up, what is the meaning of this?' she said in her best schoolmarm voice, now at the top of the stairs looking down at him, hands on hips. All the DS could do was look up at her and murmur embarrassingly about 'those bastards in there' as the muffled sound of childish giggling came from the DC's office.

As well as the fun and games, I had a reputation for hard interviewing – the Police and Criminal Evidence Act was not in force, so interviews were more intrusive and robust. It was them against us and anything went, they could not automatically have a solicitor present for the interview. It was the time when miscarriages of justice were purported to go on and, as I have said, I suppose that they must have – occasionally! What I do know is that over the period I had three separate prisoners admitting to me offences that they had not committed. In one of the cases, the PACE Act would not have helped him, in fact it would have been a definite hindrance.

I came on at 4pm to work the 4pm to midnight shift. When I arrived, the office was empty, and I phoned the DS up at Northwich to see what was happening.

'There's been a robbery in the precinct, we caught the offender and officers are dealing with him. They have had all afternoon and can't cough the bastard, get over here and get the job sorted out.'

I set off for Northwich. What had happened was that the licensee of the rough pub on one of the council estates had been putting money in the bank night safe in the town centre when a man with a pickaxe handle had attacked him and taken the money. Two women came forward and said that they had been leaving the supermarket and seen this robbery and recognised the man involved. They each named him and were quite adamant that they knew him and that he was the offender. After officers told the licensee what the women had said, he agreed with them, the named man was the robber. The named man was found in the landlord's pub playing pool and identified to the officers when they went to get him. What better evidence, two independent women witnesses and the aggrieved? During the all-afternoon interview he had denied it, no solicitors were involved and now it was my turn.

I must admit that I did put him under some robust pressure to admit the offence. (It's a good cover all word 'robust', isn't it?) But he consistently denied it. After a while he relented and said that it was him and that he had done the robbery. As usual in these circumstances, I felt great; I took a statement from him admitting the job and doubts started to creep in.

'Where is the pickaxe handle now?'

'I chopped it up.'

'Where is the money?'

'I paid a debt.'

Something was wrong here.

'You really haven't done this fucking job have you?' He then burst into tears.

'No, no, I haven't, no one will believe me and there are those witnesses.'

I finished the statement and contacted the DS.

'I've coughed him.'

'Good lad, I knew that you would.'

'Not as easy as that mate, he hasn't done it!'

'What do you mean, he hasn't done it, and you said you had coughed him.'

'I have, and he hasn't, I believe him, let's bin it.'

'We can't, there are independent witnesses, it will have to run.'

The job did run. I made my feelings known and luckily the man had a few alibi witnesses. He appeared at Crown

Court and was justly found not guilty. In these days, I doubt that he would have got off. Later, when I was on the Regional Crime Squad, I had an informant who told me that the job had been an inside one and he even named the real alleged offender. By now the licensee had a pub in Liverpool. I always felt sorry for the suspect though and realised just how easy it was to get miscarriages of justice on a much larger scale than that.

Chapter Fifteen

Accused of assault in Liverpool

STAYING ON A SIMILAR THEME, even if you weren't rough with prisoners, you could get accused of it anyway. One day I had Stewart Cookson working with me, he was on his CID Aide at the time. We had information that a motorcycle had been stolen from Winsford and the offender had been arrested in Liverpool riding it. We set off for the police station in Liverpool where we spoke with the custody sergeant.

'We've come to deal with the prisoner Sarge,' I said looking at the rather stressed and, I suspected weak, custody sergeant.

'What are you doing, are you taking him back?'

'Well, not if he's having the job, we'll deal with him here, charge and bail him.' This was the usual action to take in the circumstances.

'Well, I don't think that he will have it, he said that he'd just found it and was bringing it to the police station!'

We went down to his cell under the very watchful eyes of the back-covering sergeant.

'Are you going to have the job mate?' I asked him as he sat on his bunk.

'No, I didn't rob noffing.'

'That's OK mate, we'll take you back to Northwich then and you can tell us there.'

'I don't want to go to Northwich, I've heard about it there!'

'OK then,' said Stewart,' tell us now and you can be dealt with and bailed.'

'We are going to have a brew now, so think about it, you know the options,' I said as we left the cell and bumped into the sergeant who had been outside listening. We went to the canteen and had a cup of tea and a bun, then about 30 minutes later at the request of the sergeant we went back down to the cells. The place was in uproar and the custody sergeant was like a demented hen.

'What did you do to him?' he asked accusingly.

I looked at him in amazement, 'What do you mean; we never laid a finger on him.'

'Well, I was listening, and I didn't hear you, I must admit that. I went to his cell when you left and he was sitting with his head in his hands with blood pouring through on to the floor, you must have thumped him, I've just got to make a phone call.

'Hello sir, custody sergeant here. A very serious complaint has been made against officers from another force; I think that you should come in.' He listened for a while and then, 'Yes sir, OK sir, I will deal with it.' He had obviously been told where to go.

'That was the superintendent, oh, what am I to do?' He started running backwards and forwards like a headless chicken.

'What's going on?' I asked interrupting his panic.

'I got his mam in and sent for the police surgeon, I went and saw him again and he was in a bad way, so I cancelled the surgeon and sent for the ambulance. They came and he refused to go with them, so I have sent for the surgeon again.' The hairs started to stick up on the back of my neck. I knew that we had not touched him, but the prospect was not that straightforward and the possibility of us being arrested for assault in Liverpool was a distinct possibility. Poor Stewart didn't know whether he was coming or going.

Very soon a small middle-aged man came through the door, his pyjama bottoms sticking out of the bottom of his trousers.

'What the fuck's going on sergeant, you get me out of bed, then cancel me, then call me again. Get a grip man; I don't think that you fucking know what you're doing.'

The sergeant looked crestfallen. 'I'm sorry doctor, but this is serious.' The doctor continued doing up his trousers as he walked past the sergeant, ignoring him and heading for his office in the cell area.

Over all the shouting, the sound of an irate Liverpool woman was coming from the cells and the words 'fucking bizzies' and 'thugs' and 'your mam's here now son' could be heard echoing from the fetid room.

It went quiet for a while and then the loud powerful voice of the doctor shouted.

'Get the officers who are dealing with this man in here now.' My bottle started going as we tentatively walked to the doctor's room.

'What do you want to do with this prisoner?' he asked.

'Well, we wanted to take him to Northwich for interview doctor,' I said hesitatingly and wincing under the withering look. I felt like a schoolboy with his angry headmaster.

'OK lad, take him; I'll sign to say that he is fit for interview.' I brightened visibly.

'But what about his injury doc?' I asked.

'You are lucky that I attended lad, I dealt with this scrote a few weeks ago when he had his nose broken. I don't know what you've got at Northwich, but it has put the shits up him. He has banged his nose again making it bleed, there's fuck all wrong with him that a handkerchief won't sort out.'

'Thank you doctor,' I said, 'if only all police surgeons were like you.' I was so genuinely grateful to this man, if the prisoner had gone in the ambulance we could possibly have been in serious trouble.

I went to the sergeant who was still looking as if his career had come to an abrupt end and was no doubt planning how far into the wolf's den, he would throw us if it would save him!

'Get the little shit out for us sarge, we're taking him.' He was amazed.

'But you can't, his injury, the allegations, what am I to tell the superintendent?'

'Just get him will you, the doctor has authorised it, tell the superintendent whatever you like, he sounds like a sensible bloke!' I had little patience with this sort of wet

Nellie police officer. In the car on the way home I spoke to the prisoner.

'You've made a false allegation against us you little shit, no one will believe you next time, so you are going to have to tell the truth now, do you understand me?'

'Ok, I will,' he said sheepishly.

'Then when you have, you can walk back to Liverpool,' I said harshly.

At Northwich I ensured that the details were added to his sheet. He made a full admission and was bailed. It was very worrying at the time and taught Stewart a lesson – and me for that matter. Unfortunately, Stewart was to die suddenly at work in the Cheshire Paedophile Squad office when he was a DC. He was only in his early forties.

I said that I wished all police surgeons were like that one, which is unfair really, I have never met a bad police surgeon. They are all used to dealing with lowlife and tend to treat them accordingly.

Just to finish here on a frequently encountered problem in the naughty 1980s, being thumped during an arrest – and thumping back!

It is imperative in the police service in whatever department that if you thump someone, you must arrest him. This is not as heinous as it seems. If someone takes a swing at you, you are perfectly at liberty to defend yourself using the minimum force necessary, but if you do and don't then arrest them, you leave yourself wide open. And always remember that humans have dirty mouths! One day I was taking a statement from a doctor when she pointed at a nasty looking and obviously septic cut on my hand.

'How did you do that? It looks septic,' she asked.

'Oh, it was in a punch-up last week, we were arresting some idiots, nothing to worry about.'

A look of concern crossed her face. 'Did you do that on someone's teeth?'

'Err, yes.'

'Do you know that human teeth have far more germs on them than dog's teeth, you would have been better off being bitten by a dog.'

I looked at her sheepish as she told me off.

'Pull down your trousers and bend over the desk!' She opened her bag and took out a hypodermic syringe, which she then stuck into my bum.

But what if you have to thump someone and they bleed a lot, and you are not injured at all? Have you ever driven along and tried to thump yourself in the face at the same time? It's very difficult but if the other guy looks like a road traffic accident, you should have something to show for the altercation. That's not as hard as it seems. Once we assisted a dog handler who was struggling to hold a prisoner down in the road. We put him in the back of our car, and I sat with him. He then spat at the driver. I grabbed him by the back of the neck and shoved his head down into the foot well where he was held until we arrived at the police station. He was then removed by pre-warned and waiting officers who were there for the purpose and taken to the charge room. We followed, it was not difficult as we could follow the blood trail – his face looked as if he had gone ten rounds with Muhammad Ali in his fitter days, there was blood everywhere. I had not hit him, but I expected the foot well to be full of blood. There was nothing, not a drop, there was no blood anywhere in the car, his face had just erupted when he got out. We never did get to the bottom of it! And I never did get very used to punching myself. Your fist always seems to slow down as it gets near to its target.

Chapter Sixteen

The Number One Regional Crime Squad

QUITE OUT OF THE BLUE A DS called Phil Bowyer who had been at Northwich and was on the Regional Crime Squad phoned me one day.

'Do you fancy coming on the squad and being my partner?'

It was 1985 and I had been on Winsford CID for five years. It was time for a change, so I agreed.

I was posted to the Runcorn office of the Number One Regional Crime Squad, better known as the RCS. The RCS was a national organisation dealing mainly with serious crime that crossed force boundaries – if criminals are leaving Liverpool to commit crime in Cheshire, for instance, the Liverpool police have no real interest in them.

At that time there was no separate branch of the RCS dealing with drugs, so we dealt with that as well. The squad came under a National Co-ordinator based at New Scotland Yard who was in effect the chief constable and his 'force' was split into regions.

The North West was the Number One Region with the head office in Manchester under a detective chief superintendent, who held the title Regional Co-ordinator. There were branch offices in Liverpool, Manchester, Runcorn, Penrith, Bolton, and Hawarden in North Wales.

The National Crime Squad has now superseded the RCS although quite a bit of the original infrastructure remains.

We dressed mostly in jeans and anoraks, but I kept a change of clothes in the boot of our car so I could dress to suit the occasion when on surveillance. One of the lads even kept a full vicar's outfit with him, dog collar and cross.

This clothing and that from other cars was removed when a new branch commander arrived. He was entirely different to his predecessor and perhaps was not the best candidate for the RCS. He was nearing the end of his career, heavily built and dour with the nickname to suit his looks: Brezhnev.

As well as the covert changes of clothes that he removed from the cars, he introduced more officialdom and red tape, both handicaps to detectives dealing with informants and the darker side of police work.

The main occupation was surveillance. We would follow known criminals with the intention of catching them on the job, or the operation would be to investigate allegations of cross boundary serious crime. To this end, we were provided with powerful saloon cars, trained to advance driving standard and in surveillance: foot, mobile and static. We had the use of observation vehicles, and a motorcyclist was part of the team. We worked in pairs – a sergeant and constable working together – and in my case it was Phil and me.

Our vehicle was a Vauxhall Cavalier. The first thing you received when entering the office was a 'handle' or nickname for use on surveillance. It made car to car transmissions shorter and to the point. Mine was 'Mariner' as I had been in the Navy; others mirrored a personality trait or suchlike. When Alan Brocklehurst later joined the squad, his 'handle' was 'Badger' as in Brock the badger. When a new detective inspector arrived, he was told that he would need to get a handle, but his reply was that he had no idea what to use. This man had hygiene problems where his teeth were concerned, to such an extent that his unofficial nickname was 'Green teeth'.

One of the lads shouted from the corner. 'What about Odin boss?'

The DI thought for a moment before replying. 'Yes – Odin, the God of War, that suits my personality (it didn't!). I will be called Odin from now on.'

He was then officially titled 'Odin' on all operation orders, and anything connected with surveillance. It was only at the end of his secondment that someone with several pints inside him took 'Odin' to one side and pointed out that

'Odin' stood for Odontology – forensic dentistry – and that the whole office was aware of this throughout his secondment.

On my first meeting with the deputy coordinator, he said, 'You're supposed to be a good thief taker. My mate is part of the Manchester United FC management team. Some bastard has stolen some farm equipment from his farm, see what you can do.'

Well, that was a challenge that I thought was impossible. His mate didn't even live in Cheshire as far as I can remember. I had kept in touch with my informants and still met them regularly. I used to work very closely with informants and was prepared to go drinking and socialising with them. I prided myself on my ability to get on with anyone, either genuinely or as an actor. I arranged to meet my informant 'Billy' (for the purposes of this book all my informants are called 'Billy') in a country pub in Cheshire. I took Phil with me, and we met up.

After getting the drinks in, I asked him if there was anything that we may be interested in. I pointed out that in this new job I had more access to 'reward' money – we tended not to call it 'snout money' when we were with snouts!

'Are you interested in the theft of farm equipment?' he asked.

I looked at him in disbelief and then at Phil to see if I was being set up. His face was blank.

Yes, it was stolen from the Manchester United man. I promised him some payment for the info if it was good and we later passed it on to local officers to deal with. They carried out the arrests and then got back to me.

'Your snout's a bit of a knob!'

'Why, the job was right, you've locked up on it!'

'That's right Paul, we did. The problem is, your snitch was one of the main men, and his associates blew him out as soon as they were arrested!'

He never got any money for that information after all, and I saw the boss soon after.

'You know that bit of a job you gave me boss?' I said smirking. 'Well, it's sorted.'

He didn't believe it. Like me, he thought I would never get anywhere and had only been messing about when he gave it to me. Still, this little job did my credibility no harm at all albeit that it was pure luck!

It is acceptable for informants to go on jobs, so long as they are not setting them up (usually they are asked to drive or keep watch). There are strict rules and consent from a senior officer has to be applied for if the intention is for an informant to take part in a crime. He then becomes a 'participating informant'.

Likewise, all informants must be registered and given a nom-de-plume. Every time they are spoken to, a form must go in. It did not really interfere with detective work; it did however protect you against spurious allegations.

Things had started to change anyway.

The first time I paid out 'snout money' the boss gave it to me and told me to only give him half and put the other half in my desk! The explanation was that if I gave it all to him, he would expect that every time, whereas if I gave him half, he would be grateful, and I could then give him the rest for more information later without the hassle of applying for it. Common sense really, but it left you wide open for potentially serious allegations! The money paid to informants varied depending on the job and for a serious job it could go up quite high, especially if the company or person benefitting from the success could be prepared to pay towards it.

The advanced driving course was the same one as traffic officers do. In fact, we all take the same course – they are wearing smart police uniforms, talking sensibly and not drinking and we are looking like tramps, taking the piss all the time, and drinking every night. Two different breeds put together, but we all got on well. The driving is done in unmarked powerful police cars with a plaque on the back saying that the car is being used for police driver training.

Most of the time is spent driving fast, especially on motorways when speeds well in excess of 100 mph are recorded. The idea is to keep to the speed limits until the de-restricted sign comes up, or in police parlance the GLF (go like fuck) sign. That is the white circle with the black stripe on it. It means that vehicles can now reach the legal maximum speed limit. In the case of the police driving school cars, they can be driven as fast as they can within the training.

The same applies to the motorway. It is on this course that you see even more than usual bad, know-it-all drivers. I am talking about the middle lane sitters and the 'I'm doing seventy miles an hour, that's quite fast enough for the outside lane' types. When they are playing the 70 in a 70-limit game in the outside lane, they look in the mirror, see the car flash at them, note that the driver has a civilian jacket on then put up two fingers and point towards the speedometer. When you look in your mirror at a following car, you tend to only see the driver, even when the car is full. It is then necessary to flash them again with one quick flash. If after two or three times they do not respond, you overtake them carefully on the inside. As you pass their faces are a picture – they scowl at you, put up two fingers and possibly tap their heads to indicate madness. Then as your car continues passing, they would see the three police uniforms with their own scowling faces atop. Their heads would then swivel quickly to the front and as soon as you completed the manoeuvre and pulled back into the fast lane, displaying the police sign on the rear, they would quickly go to the nearside lane where they would probably stay for the rest of their motoring life.

These idiots, who are usually middle-aged men, could just as easily be interfering with a live and very important surveillance on terrorists or suchlike. It's not only the police who do this; operations involving the Secret Service and Customs, for instance, are all put at risk by these clever sods.

After the advanced course comes the surveillance course. Now, the daft driving really starts. You drive like a duck swims. When you are near the target vehicle that you are following, you drive sedately and observe all the rules. When you leave the target and have to catch up anything goes, you drive very fast in unmarked cars with everyone thinking that you are a hooligan. To leave the front of a five or six car surveillance without being seen means turning off somewhere, allowing the whole convoy to pass when they are spread out over a mile or so, and then trying to catch up in heavy traffic. All the time we would be on car-to-car radio with the 'eyeball' car giving a running commentary.

Rushing to catch up and being helped by the other cars would leave innocent motorists amazed. The car ahead could call you through for instance going around sharp hairpin bends, or over the brow of a hill by telling you that the road is clear. All the car that you are overtaking into the blind bend can see is a total lunatic. There is also training in foot surveillance.

Not long after my joining the squad, Phil returned to divisional CID work and I joined a new partner, Paul Sinclair, a well-built officer who was a character in the nicest sense of the word. He was quite unique, a detective sergeant from Liverpool who was both streetwise and naïve at the same time. He would do anything to help anyone and was an excellent friend as well as a work colleague.

Our office contained officers from Liverpool and Cheshire with a constable from Manchester. It was a good, happy office with a modicum of success.

This next story is probably the most successful operation that the office undertook during my first period on the RCS.

Chapter Seventeen

Undercover on a successful drugs operation

THE CHESHIRE DRUG SQUAD was also based at Runcorn, and we had done a few jobs with them. They had an answerphone on all of the time; I think that it was called 'Drug Watch'. It was a facility whereby anyone could phone the number and pass information on drug dealing. In February 1986, someone phoned to say that a lad from Warrington, by the name of John Buckley, was dealing in drugs in the area with drugs he was buying from a dealer in Oldham.

The information was very good and detailed; it was enhanced by means of surveillance. The information included the fact that the main Oldham dealer, Richard Hunt, who originated from Warrington, would drive to Hartshead Moor service station on the M62 near Bradford. He would then await a phone call on one of the public phones, answer it (this was well before everyone had a mobile phone), and then drive to a petrol station just off the motorway in Bradford.

At the petrol station, a man of Asian origin would stop and drive off. Hunt would follow him into an industrial estate or on to the moors where the drugs would change hands. A vast quantity of drugs. Hunt dealt to dealers and his unknown supplier was a step further up the line. Our aim, or wishful thinking, was to get to the top of the dealing chain and, if possible, the importers.

An operation was set up and given the name Operation Atherton. We were split into teams for the initial evidence-gathering period: two officers from the Cheshire drug squad, two from the Manchester branch office of the RCS and Paul and I from the Runcorn branch office. Together we made up the nucleus of the operation. We also split the duties of the respective teams.

One team carried out static observations on the rear of Hunt's flat in Queens Road, Oldham. This was a ground floor flat at the back of a large pair of Victorian semi-detached houses. The same landlord owned them, and a door had been knocked through, to make it one large house containing thirteen flats or bedsits, some bigger than others. Across the road from the rear of these premises there was a large red brick office block that had once housed an insurance company by the name of Minster Insurance. The premises were now empty and up for sale, and we took over the second storey as an observation point.

Each time we entered; we relieved the previous team. We had the use of a video camera on a tripod, which was aimed at the rear yard of the suspect premises. Whilst one team was engaged on this, another team went to the service station to await the arrival of Hunt. The third team carried out mobile inquiries and observations on other premises. We could call on other teams for back-up or surveillance purposes.

The observations at the rear of the flat were boring, but the Hartshead Moor operation took some beating. Observations went on there daily for a few weeks. Motorway services are just about tolerable if you're stopping for a ten-minute break, but to sit for eight hours at a time is mind-numbing. The only relief was a stroll through the shop and gaming arcade, but we soon grew tired of looking at magazines, cheap cassette tapes and pies. To make matters worse, we later discovered that this part of the operation had been a complete waste of time.

The Obs on the flat were going better. We saw many comings and goings at the rear, and even saw and videoed a burglary at the flat – he got in through a small window and it was later discovered that he had stolen a few hundred pounds. What we didn't have was a view to the front. The front door looked out on to a relatively quiet road, and then out onto an expanse of park. There was just nowhere to get a safe observation spot.

I went and saw the DI. 'What about me getting a bedsit in there boss?' I said. 'One of the ground floor rooms at the front is empty.'

'What, move in there yourself?'

'Yeah, why not? It's the only way to see the front door, and we're losing a lot of intelligence.'

He eventually agreed to it although my partner, Paul, was a bit dubious and thought I'd get sussed out and murdered. I got an old Royal Navy suitcase from home and went to see Mr Mir, the landlord.

'I believe that you have some bedsits for rent,' I said. 'I've just come out of the Navy and me missus has picked her time well; she's just left me. I just need somewhere to sort my head out.'

'There's one down the road,' he said. 'It's £60 a month, with a month in advance. Can you manage that?'

'Yes,' I replied, hoping that in the cash-strapped police force I would get reimbursed. I walked down with him, and he took me to a nice large upstairs room above Hunt's own flat. But it was at the rear.

'This is a good one,' said Mr Mir, helpfully. 'It has got an en-suite.'

'What about at the front?' I said. 'There's a nice view of the park.'

'There is one,' he said. 'But it's just a room with a sink. This is far better.'

I had to think fast. 'Well, can I have that one cheaper?'

'No,' he said. 'Sorry. But I don't mind showing it to you.'

The room at the front was smelly and scruffy, but it had a brilliant view of the front path.

'This will do me fine,' I said, hoping I wasn't arousing any suspicions with this apparent insanity. I just had to have that room.

'Okay,' he said, dubiously. 'Suit yourself. I'll bring you a rent book in a while. But I want the deposit tomorrow.'

It was only after I left it that I found out that the previous tenant, a drug user, had collapsed over a two-bar electric fire and cooked on it for quite a while before his body was found. That perhaps explained some of the smell.

When Mr Mir left, I took out my covert radio. 'Mariner to Spectrum!' I said, Paul's handle was Spectrum after Spectrum Computers.

No, answer from Paul. I tried again. Nothing. Shit. Now I was worried that the flat was in a radio black spot and would be useless for its purpose. I left and walked down to where he was parked.

I soon realised why he hadn't replied.

I opened the door and shouted, 'What d'you think you're doing?'

He nearly jumped out of his skin.

'What!? What's up?' he said, looking up like a startled bush baby.

'You were asleep you bastard!' I said. 'I've been calling you.'

'I wasn't, I was just resting my eyes,' he said, sheepishly.

'Well, I've got that room, and I'm going back to try again. So don't rest your eyes this time.'

The reception was perfect. With Paul in the other observation spot, I spent the next few weeks settling in and getting to know some of the other residents. My immediate neighbour was an old man, and we'd spend time together chatting about nonsense. Most of the other tenants were young lads, and I would often go with them to the pub at the bottom of the road and play pool. I was supposed to be living there, and many nights I stayed; when I thought I could get away with it, I left late and went home to my wife and kids, returning early the following day.

Ritchie Hunt kept to himself, and I had little to do with the rest of my neighbours. Other than that, I was gradually getting more unkempt, smelly, and unshaven every day, and was soon accepted as one of the lads. And, with my view to the front, we could see a lot more. People were coming to buy drugs quite frequently and each incident was recorded with the time and date. One regular customer, who would turn up in a new convertible sports car, was Andy Rourke, the bass guitarist from The Smiths, a very successful pop group at the time. He drove a fancy top of the range Ford Escort, Buckley himself would arrive in his black Ford Capri from time to time, but the job was not coming together. The motorway services side was going nowhere, and it looked like all we were going to end up with was a couple of minor dealers. We couldn't justify continuing an expensive op like this for much longer for a catch of that size.

About six weeks in, the boss DI Les Lee called a meeting.

'We can't go on much longer,' he said. 'If the Hartshead Moor info is wrong, the rest could be. We'll have to hit the flat.'

We couldn't argue. By now, we knew who the regular callers were, and it looked like there was little more to be gained. It was planned that we would hit the flat on Friday 11 April 1986. We'd get Buckley and Hunt and wrap as many other fish as possible in the net.

Chapter Eighteen

Strike day is the operation is a success?

I WAS IN MY FLAT ON STRIKE DAY, with a large team from the drug squad and the RCS on standby at Longsight police station awaiting my call.

I looked out and saw that Buckley's Capri was already outside. That was enough. I contacted Longsight, and people started to make their way over. The idea was that some officers would covertly join me in my flat and would be close at hand when the order to strike was given. The others would be in the insurance office and in cars nearby. At 12.20pm, Alan Brocklehurst and other detectives joined me. Not long after this, Andy Rourke arrived in his convertible and went to Hunt's flat. It was then decided that when either Buckley or Rourke left, they would be arrested in the garden and the raid would commence.

By now we had suspicions that Rourke was himself a dealer though it later turned out that he was not – and if we were right then the odds were he'd have a significant quantity of heroin on him. The same was certainly true of Buckley. Whoever left first was potentially going down for a lengthy stretch, while the one who stayed in the flat would have time to drop any drugs he had received. Without knowing it, one of them was about to make one of the most important decisions of his life.

Buckley lost. At 2.45pm he came out of the flat and the order to execute the warrants was given. He was arrested in the garden and, when searched, he had in his possession 18.3 grams of heroin with a street value of £1,830, for which he later received a heavy prison sentence. As the officers entered Hunt's flat, Rourke stuffed down the side of the settee 1.1 grams of heroin with a street value of £70. He denied being a supplier but admitted that he had a £500-per-week habit, and later received a two-year suspended sentence and a fine. He had been driving to Oldham for his drugs as he thought it was safer than Moss Side.

Also arrested at the house were a chap called Jonathan Makin and one of my fellow residents, Robert Heap. Both were drug dealers in their own right. I was with Paul and Brocky, together with some others, and we searched Heap's flat. Paul told him that I was a detective, not just a neighbour, and after a bit of persuasion he agreed to show us where the drugs were. In all 15.1 grams of heroin were recovered valued at £1,200 which he claimed he was looking after for Hunt. A later search of the loft in his father's house in Oldham revealed a cash box containing £18,185, and £137 in cheques made out to Vanilla Fudge. Most of the money belonged to Hunt, and Vanilla Fudge was a hairdresser's shop that he had rented in Tib Street, Manchester.

Hunt's Toyota Celica car had a secret compartment behind the dashboard for carrying drugs, and when his flat was searched 291.43 grams of heroin were found, worth nearly £30,000. He later admitted to dealing in about £1.8 million-worth of heroin over the previous two years and got a long prison sentence.

But on the day of the raid, we didn't feel we'd got much in the way of a result.

'Well, that's it?' I said to Brocky, my good mate and partner for the day. 'Bit of an anti-climax, after all that work. Okay, we've some drugs and some money, and a couple of prisoners, but did it justify the work?'

The four prisoners had been taken to Warrington police station, and we were back in my flat. We'd decided to spend the rest of the day there, just to see if any more dealers came to Hunt's flat to buy. A DC from the Hawarden RCS office was in there to answer the door, along with Hunt's girlfriend Yvette, their young son and Rourke's girlfriend Michelle, who was very attractive indeed. The young boy was one thing that made me feel it had been worth it: he was a lovely little lad, and he was living in absolute squalor, surrounded by the filth and sordid way of life the drug dealing seems to bring.

'So much for the Pakistani main man,' said Alan. 'It looks like we'll just have Hunt.'

We carried on being miserable, only cheering ourselves up by draping a condom over the DC's pipe when he came to my room for a sociable smoke. He sat reading an old copy of *Mad* magazine that he'd found under my bed and puffed away contentedly for some time. He was there for a while before he realised what we'd done, at which point he launched himself off the bed like a rocket, condom, pipe and magazine flying everywhere.

He had not long gone back to Hunt's flat, calling us a pair of twats, when the radio suddenly burst into life, making me and Brocky jump. It was just coming up to 10pm, the time we had arranged to call it a day.

It was the DC.

'Lads,' he said. 'Get in here, there's two callers.'

We went through and standing in the room were two Pakistani men.

'What have you come here for?' I asked.

'Nothing,' said one of them, bowing his head.

'You must be here for something.'

'We've come with a video, sir,' he said. 'My friend has a business.'

What a load of rubbish, I thought. *I wonder... No, that's too much to hope for.*

We'd had quite a bit of luck here, but what were the odds of these being the main men? I arrested them anyway – their names were Mohammed Khan and Tariq Mahmood Rafiq – and we escorted them to my flat. I left them with Alan to arrange transport and went back to speak with Hunt's girlfriend.

'Do you know them, Yvette?' I asked.

'Well, the tall one's been here before,' she said.

That was Khan. 'What do you know about him?'

'Ritchie told me that he's the person who his dealer buys his gear from,' she said with a shrug. 'That's about all I can say.'

I could have kissed her. *Yes! Yes! Yes!* I said to myself, barely able to contain my excitement. She'd said plenty enough for me!

I pulled myself together and asked the Hawarden DC to get me something in writing from Yvette. Soon, the transport arrived, and the two men were taken to Warrington. As soon as they were gone, I told Alan the good news and, after dancing around the room hugging each other, we made our way back to Warrington. We were perhaps a little premature, but not much.

Surely, this job could not get any better now.

At Warrington, the team had gone into the Patten Arms pub next door to celebrate what they thought was a reasonable job.

'Guess who's just been lodged in the cells?' said Alan, to the room in general.

'Go on,' someone replied sarcastically. 'You'll be telling us next it's the Pakistani main man.'

When it dawned on them that two men *had* been arrested, quite possibly the main men, the party really started.

The following day, Brocky and I interviewed Khan. He was aged about thirty, and from Bradford, religious and very polite, even servile of manner. He started with a load of rubbish about wanting to buy a flat and seeing people going in to that one. I did the talking and Alan wrote down the questions and answers. After this increasingly silly story had gone on for a while, I said, 'Look, let's not play games. We're investigating the supply and use of drugs, and we believe you are involved. I want you to consider carefully before you answer. You might end up having to swear to the truth about this on the Koran.'

He thought about it for a minute or two. Finally, he said, 'Okay. I could never lie on the Koran.'

We got him a cup of tea and the interview proper commenced.

'When did you first meet Ritchie Hunt?'

'About five or six months ago.'

'Who were you with?'

'Karam Dad Khan.'

From there he coughed the lot. Karam Dad Khan – known as KD – turned out to be the man we wasted weeks waiting for at Hartshead Moor Services. Unbeknown to us, they had changed arrangements just prior to the start of our op. Karam Dad Khan was a full-time dealer, with our Khan and Tariq Mahmood Rafiq employed as go-betweens. They'd been regular suppliers of Ritchie, getting a few hundred quid for their troubles, and had been in the process of cutting KD out of the deal after being introduced to one of *his* suppliers, a middle-aged Nigerian woman they'd met at a house in Bradford. She used the name Fatima, he said, was wearing African dress and regularly came up from London on the train.

The most recent deal she'd done was for heroin worth £6,000.

'Can you tell us anything more about her?' I asked.

'No, I've told you everything, sir.'

I didn't believe him – who buys significant weight of drugs off someone they know nothing about? – but he passed on details of some other suppliers, and it looked like we'd have to be content with that.

Meanwhile, Tariq Mahmood Rafiq had been interviewed by other detectives, had admitted nothing, and had been released on police bail. Alan and myself later went to Bradford to re-arrest him, obtained a full admission and he and Mohammed Khan eventually received lengthy prison sentences.

We started acting on the other information we'd extracted from Khan – members of the team visited Leicester and Hull and had a lot of success. But our mystery Nigerian woman remained an enigma.

The following week I went back to my flat in Oldham with the Warrington photographer and scenes of crime man, Fred Clare, to record all the places where drugs and money had been found. From an investigative point of view, the job was pretty much finished – it was just a matter of tying up the loose ends.

We got in, took some pictures – including a couple of snaps of me standing beside my smelly old bed for posterity – and I was thinking of making a move when Fred called me over.

'Look at this,' he said, looking out of the window. 'Where does she think she's going? Some carnival or something?'

'Eh?' I said.

'There's some woman out there in a taxi. She's wearing some sort of national dress.'

A shiver went down my back. Fred knew nothing about the Nigerian, so he couldn't be taking the piss. I hurried over and looked out. Sure enough, there she was, in a long, flowing, multi-coloured robe and some sort of turban.

I went out to meet her, only to see Alan Brocklehurst step out of a car which had just pulled up behind hers. It was pure luck, but it meant he beat me to the punch. Alan had no idea and had not been following her, it was just a coincidence, he was coming to visit me!

'Is your name Fatima and are you from London?' he said.

'Yes, my dear,' she said, shyly. She stood out a bit because of her appearance, but otherwise she came over as a very ordinary middle-aged woman, one who spent her days as a housewife and mother.

'I am arresting you on suspicion of the importation and supply of Class A controlled drugs,' said Alan, with a sly look at me. He knew full well that he was stealing my rather prestigious prisoner. At this, the nice, shy middle-aged lady became a psychopath and started to struggle violently. And not surprisingly – we later found that she had secreted 270.5 grams of heroin in five egg-shaped wraps about her person.

Back then, that had a street value of around £27,000, a significant amount of cash and drugs, in today's money £85,919.34.

The next time we saw 'Fatima' – real name Binta Ofili – was at Mold Crown Court in North Wales, where she was found guilty of dealing drugs and duly sentenced. She hardly flinched as the judge spoke, and I was just thinking that fair play, she was a pretty cool customer, when there was a blood-curdling scream from the cells. We later learned that she'd said to the gaolers on the way down, 'That wasn't bad, I expected more than eighteen months.'

'Eighteen months?' said one. 'He gave you eighteen *years.*'

Then she screamed.

So, Operation Atherton turned out very nicely indeed: seventeen people were charged with various offences and long prison sentences were meted out in what was the most successful police drugs operation in the north of England to that point. Everyone involved was commended, including the Manchester officer whose only involvement had been in operating the video from the office block at the rear. He had filmed the strike and had taped over the film that we had taken of a burglary at the flat! Not that it mattered. The professional satisfaction involved in a job like that was immense.

Chapter Nineteen

Welsh Robbers & 'rescued by Scallys'

LIFE CARRIED ON with an operation in Rhyl on a team of armed robbers. It was scary stuff – during the surveillance, they'd been seen through a window waving a sawn-off shotgun around. We split into two shifts to give round the clock cover, with a North Wales firearms team always standing by for back-up and a firearms officer on each shift. I took the job on our shift, wearing a .38 Smith & Wesson Special on my belt under my anorak. It's a strange feeling, walking around a holiday resort, playing the fruit machines in the arcades, with a loaded gun heavy on your hip. I was a qualified firearms officer, not the type that goes out looking like Darth Vader but qualified to carry a gun.

After a while, never having caught them carrying out a robbery, it was decided to arrest them anyway. Their car was stopped in the middle of Connah's Quay in front of a bus full of pensioners. The main man wasn't in their vehicle, so we set out to his home address, which was No17 in a quiet street in Rhyl. We dispatched one of the footmen to identify the house, and he came back and indicated that it was the first one down a narrow entry.

It was all highly efficient. Up roared several big white Ford Granadas full of Welsh firearms officers in black boiler suits and flak jackets, armed with various weapons. A dozen barrels were instantly trained on the property, including a machine gun on a tripod, and the first attempt was made to smash in the door.

At which the one next door opened, and an old lady appeared, looking puzzled.

'I dawn't think Missus Jawns is a criminal,' she said, in a soft Welsh lilt. 'She's ninety if she's a day. Lovely old lady, so she is, out shopping I think, with her daughter.'

It turned out there was another No17, which was eventually located by a Merseyside firearms man, me, and the superintendent in charge of the RCS operation.

'We'd better go and tell the cavalry,' said the superintendent.

'We don't want that performance again,' said my mate.

'You go and tell them boss,' I said to the superintendent, with a wink. 'We'll have a look around here.'

'On your heads be it,' he said, knowingly, 'but be careful.'

As he beat a diplomatic retreat, we kicked in the front door and took a room each. The spooky bit in these jobs is going upstairs: if anyone pops a gun over the top of the banister, you're very vulnerable. I remember at one point getting down on my knees to look under a bed, and placing my gun hand, finger on the trigger, on the bed to steady myself. As I came back up, I remembered an incident from not long before. A police firearms man had been leaning on a bed with a cocked weapon in just that manner, and as he straightened back up the weapon had discharged – hitting a child whom he was not aware was there. It dawned on me that I could easily have done the same, and that I'd have been right in the firing line for the Shudder Squad – those senior officers, lawyers and people in armchairs who will never have to do these jobs themselves but who can't wait to tell you what you 'shudder' done differently. When you're looking for armed and dangerous men, these considerations shouldn't be in your mind, but unfortunately, they are. We seldom got involved with dealing with the prisoners after the arrest, just handing them over. On this occasion we did neither, it was left to the Welsh officers.

By now? 1984, I was involved in surveillance instructing. The foot surveillance course was usually done in Liverpool city centre, and quite often I acted as the 'hare'. The students had to follow me around the town and remember everything that I did using the procedures that they had been taught in the classroom. I wouldn't be expected to deliberately mislead them, but at the same time, they had to be tested. In order that the day would not be wasted if one of them got lost, there would be an arrangement to pass a certain landmark every hour or so. They were expected to come into shops and suchlike with me, but often they would wait outside and that enabled me to lose some of them. I would often go into a certain bank which has a door on one street but another at the back into St Johns Market. If they didn't follow me, they had lost me and would be penalised for it.

On one occasion, I had a newly posted and quite strait-laced DCI tailing me. There was a sex shop on Lime Street – a tiny place, with room for only one or two customers. This was a good test. I went in and, quite rightly, he followed.

'Have you got any of those bendy vibrators?' I asked the assistant. The DCI stood almost alongside me in the cramped interior, looking very hot under the collar. In no time at all, I had a row of dildos buzzing and bobbing about on the counter. While I was playing, the assistant asked the DCI if he could help him. He did quite well and asked for some Durex, but then he had to leave. It might sound like I was messing around, but it was good training. He'd been inside, he knew there was no other exit and so he could safely wait for me to come out.

One sneaky trick – you'll have seen it in lots of films – was to stand by the automatic doors on the Merseyrail train, the footmen discreetly watching me. As the doors hissed prior to shutting, I needed only to move my shoulder slightly to have them all jumping off and standing forlornly on the platform as the train pulled out of the station with me on it.

A lot of it is about thinking on your feet. Some struggle more with this than others. On one occasion I got into a department store lift and a footman followed me. With my hand hovering over the buttons, I said, 'What floor do you want mate?'

'Er... three,' he said, nervously.

I really enjoyed pointing out to him that we were already on that floor and he got out quickly.

In a place like Liverpool, where there are eyes everywhere, it's important to remember that it's not just your target who might see you.

I was just leaving Liverpool Central station one day when I found myself being dragged backwards into a taxi outside by some well-meaning scallywags.

'The fucken' bizzies are following you, mate,' said one of them. 'We was watching them, the fucken' pricks!'

They pulled me down onto the floor of the cab and told the driver to get going.

'What 'ave yer fucken' done, mate?'

'Been doin' a birra fucken kyting (bouncing credit cards),' I said from the floor, in my best Scouse. 'Burra didn't know the twats was onto us.'

They dropped me off half a mile further on. 'Thanks lads,' I said, 'I owe yer one.'

'No problem, mate,' said one of them. 'We've gorra fucken' stick together against them bastads.'

I climbed out of the taxi and saw my crime squad trainees in a taxi some distance behind on the other side of the road. *Full marks for that*, I thought. Like I say – thinking on your feet is important during surveillance, and it only comes with practice.

On one occasion, doing it for real, we were following a team of armed robbers and lost them near a gun shop in Chester. The shop was attached to a commercial shooting range and set in its own grounds. We suspected that they might be heading there anyway, so I went inside. What I didn't know was that some soft-in-the-head member of our team had already been in and identified himself to the proprietor five minutes earlier, asking if the bloke had seen their car.

As I walked in, I immediately saw the suspects in there – one looking at a shotgun and the other picking up some ammunition.

The proprietor looked up. 'Hello, mate,' he said to me. 'Are you from the police? I've just seen one of your lads.'

The hairs stood up on the back of my neck, and suddenly the targets were taking a lot of notice.

'Yes,' I said to the proprietor, with my back to them, winking furiously. 'I was wondering if there's a range free on Saturday. The Chester police team need a bit of practice for a competition?'

He was quick, realised what was happening, and answered me well. I left the shop and kept away from them thereafter.

Around that time there was a brilliant demonstration of what can be achieved with good surveillance. The Provisional IRA had been observed by the Met anti-terrorist squad unloading firearms and explosives from a boat on the Welsh coast. They had also been seen setting up arms dumps in Delamere Forest and Macclesfield Forest. I was part of the team tasked with watching the dump in Delamere one night. We were strictly forbidden from going anywhere near it. The Provos had sunk a plastic dustbin into the ground, placed the weapons and explosives inside, and sealed it with tape. The bin was then covered over and the area well camouflaged, with traps left so that they could tell if anyone had been near it.

None of us was armed, my ticket having expired, and I never bothered renewing it. It wasn't much fun, knowing that you were near a terrorist arms dump to which they might return, heavily-armed, at any time. But it was all quiet – apart from one incident, when a tramp wandered out of the darkness from the direction of the dump. I arrested him and checked him out at length, and he was clean. The following night, a firearms officer was attached, and the terrorists were eventually arrested and sent away for very long terms.

Chapter Twenty

Good Detective / Bent Detective?

THERE'S A FINE LINE to be trod in my line of business as far as informants are concerned. Most of them are active criminals, and it is tempting for detectives to want to turn a blind eye to their own man's involvement in crime in order to keep him out and about and passing information on. This sometimes means operations must be kept secret from other police officers, lest they yield to this temptation.

I recall one job we did in Liverpool which we didn't inform the local cops about. It was a 'long firm fraud', where you set up in business with no intention of paying your suppliers. The main man was informing for officers in the city, and regularly socialised with them, so our operation was all very hush-hush.

The baddies had rented a factory unit on an industrial estate in St Helens, along with a bank of telephones and fax machines, some office furniture, and a forklift truck. They assumed a company name, and their first purchase was a load of goods from two firms, which were paid for in full. They also deposited a few thousand pounds in a local bank. This created the illusion of honesty – they could use these firms and the bank as references to secure future prospective clients, to get them to extend a line of credit. The firms in this second wave would *not* be getting paid.

One member of the gang had a string of shops which sold cheap bits and bobs along with loose goods on a weigh-it-yourself type basis, which was where the stuff they ordered would be sold on.

We plotted up nearby and were soon watching salesmen turning up, keen to sell to the new firm and completely taken in by appearances – it all looked perfectly legit, with men working and a 'depot manager' busy at his rented desk. Next, we saw truckloads of goods turn up – the gang took delivery of virtually anything that can be sold dry and loose in barrels, together with lots of shelf stock... disposable nappies, rolls of bin liners, that kind of thing.

As soon as the big wagons were unloaded into the premises and had left, small vans would turn up and take the stuff away. We would follow them to the gang member's shops, recording every trip they made.

It's a surprisingly easy scam. You order your goods and stall on paying the invoice. Eventually, after a month or two, the supplier enters the lumbering legal process, with solicitor's letters and suchlike pinging around. But these things take time, and while one firm may decide to cut off its dealings there is a constant stream of others ready to take its place.

Some firms suffered heavily and were nearly put out of business, including the Wrexham firm who supplied the nappies and a Midlands company which made the bin-liners.

What usually happens – as the ponderous wheels of justice finally grind round towards the day of reckoning – is that the criminals either torch the building and disappear, or just empty it and remove evidence of their presence. They can then start up again somewhere else. If you get away with it a few times, you have the capital, knowledge, and infrastructure required to become legitimate; at least one once well-known supermarket chain started in this way (They have since been bought out and no longer exist).

On this occasion, we struck first, and they were all arrested, and then bailed. The main man, who was the brains behind it all, denied all knowledge of the chap who owned the shops, and vice versa, and there was frustratingly little evidence to implicate him. Christmas came and went, and it was decided to arrest the main man again.

Among the arrest team was a Liverpool DS, whom I'll call Mike.

'You wait here,' he said, when we got to the address – an expensive house in an affluent part of Liverpool. 'I know him, and I'll deal with him.'

I watched him trudge to the front door.

'This job is a cock up,' I told Paul, as we waited in the drive. 'I hope he's searching it properly. There could be Christmas cards in there from one to the other to prove association between him and the fella with the shops.'

'He knows what he's doing,' said Paul, protectively. Paul Sinclair was a very trusting soul.

While we waited, I had a stroll around the garden. On looking through the garage window, I thought I was seeing things. It was full of the bin-liners and nappies that had been supplied to the gang. He had obviously been stupid and kept them for his own use.

I removed the boxes and put them by our cars, then went into the house to check that Mike was doing his job properly. I found him waiting patiently at the bottom of the stairs for the main man to get ready.

'His garage is full of hooky gear,' I said.

Mike just shrugged it off.

I was pursuing my other theory, and checking the Christmas cards on the sideboard, when the main man came downstairs.

'What the fuck's he doing in my house?' he said, arrogantly, to Mike.

'I'm searching it,' I said. 'With a warrant. And I've found your nappies and bin-liners.'

At that, we all walked outside. Mike was clearly angry. 'Will you get this twat out of here, Paul,' he said, pointing at me.

'Oh, dear me,' I said, grinning. 'Am I upsetting your close friend?'

We got the main man into a car and away, and when it all came to trial the only real evidence, we had against him was the nappies and bin bags. It was enough, though: he went to prison.

I took the opportunity to have a word with Mike at the Warrington canteen over breakfast one morning.

'Don't you ever fucking talk to me like that again,' I said. 'I don't care how close you get to these shits, but don't involve me.'

I'm not saying he was properly corrupt, but he had certainly allowed his personal relationship with the main man to override his professionalism. It's not unusual. It has always amazed me how wealthy and 'senior' villains are treated with respect by some members of the police and prison service – as if they deserve that respect. I've always seen them as the lowlife that they are, the damage they do to decent society far outweighs that done by the insignificant nobodies who make up the majority of the criminal element.

Saying that, I can understand how it happens. I got on well with a lot of my informants, and it made the job easier. You just have to remember who you are, and who they are. Fortunately, none of my snouts ever owned a yacht in the Med or dated models; a week's holiday in a rancid tower block in Liverpool or 'a go at me missus' never really appealed to me.

And when you don't like them, you pretend you do. A good detective is part actor, part salesman. The salesmanship comes in when you're persuading them to admit to their crimes. Some of the people I worked with could have sold snow to Eskimos – it's harder to get a man to admit to something that will send him to prison than it is to get him to buy a car he doesn't need. You'll use similar techniques with magistrates, when you are interceding with them behind locked doors, looking for clemency for the bloke you've just had convicted. I did this a few times – ask to see them in their retiring room and tell them, off the record, why your informant should receive preferential treatment. The friendship means laughing at their jokes when you're out drinking with them and ruffling their kids' hair when you call round to see them at home.

Another thing to bear in mind is that your informants' real mates won't know you're Old Bill. I was at Billy's one afternoon, and he told me where some stolen property was.

'I'll take you round there if you like?' he said.

We jumped in my car – an old red Regional Crime Squad Peugeot, which had been the only vehicle available that day. Covert RCS cars were fitted with car-to-car and main set radios, operated by a floating cable with a button or switch on the end and a switch on the dashboard. To talk, you just pressed one of the switches and everything was picked up by the concealed mike. This car was about to be sold, so everything should have been stripped out of it (it also meant that I was completely out of touch – health and safety officers eat your hearts out!).

We set off through deepest Liverpool. Suddenly, Billy shouted. 'There's me mate! Stop a minute, Paul.'

I pulled over and he ran back to a man standing on the footpath. I waited for a minute and then saw Billy coming back with his friend.

'Eh, Paul,' he said. 'Can we just give Danny a lift? He wants to go and score in Tocky.'

For normal readers, this meant Danny wanted to go and buy drugs in Toxteth.

Without waiting for an answer, they both jumped in.

'Cheers mate, you're a fucken' star!' said Danny, settling himself into the back seat of the scruffy Peugeot like royalty.

I set off, Billy chattering away, me throwing in the odd comment, until Danny suddenly blurted out, 'What the fuck's this?'

We both looked round. He was holding one of the microphones leads that had been left in.

Head for thinking, feet for dancing, I thought. Depending on my reply, Billy's Street Cred could take a dangerous bashing here.

But he was thinking quicker than I was. 'You're getting a free ride in a fucken' taxi,' he said. 'That's the radio mike.'

Danny still looked quizzical.

'That *was* the radio mike,' I said, indicating the brackets in the glove compartment that had held the 'radio.' 'The fucken' car's going for sale and the radio has gone from the other end. That's where we're off now, the auction.'

'It's not in bad nick, is it?' said Danny, looking round him and prodding things. Fortunately, he was not a genius. 'What will it fetch, I might be interested?'

'Nah, it's booked in,' I said, hoping he'd let it drop. I'd pulled some tricks but selling squad cars to druggies was too far. Luckily, we dropped him off on a council estate in Toxteth not long afterwards.

I was with an office DS when we worked on a blackmail case. Someone had sent letters to Kellogg's in Manchester demanding £10,000, or their products would be contaminated. It wasn't much, but they were to put the money in a sealed box marked 'Undeveloped X rays, do not open' and have an employee take it to the Hop Pole pub in Warrington town centre and wait there with it. We plotted up on the pub with footmen inside. We'd been there a while and it was getting very close to closing time, but nothing had happened, and I was just writing it off as another wild goose chase when a man picked the box up off the table.

The footmen had stayed just about sober enough to follow him out to his car, where they took his registration number and radioed us with his direction of travel. We followed it to the Irish Club in Warrington and saw the driver get out and walk to the door to find it closed. He then drove to a semi-detached house on a typical private estate. We were first there and gave the order to strike. We ran into the house, my partner Terry Oates went upstairs after the man, while I grabbed the woman who had been in the car and was his wife and the money in the hall.

We were not involved in interviewing them, but this is what happened: the woman did not speak for two days, but after a day the man confessed that he had been paid by a man with an Irish accent to collect a parcel from the pub. He was not told what it was, but suspected it was a gun or something. He said he was only going to be a courier for one of the terrorist organisations.

This was rubbish. It was a scam thought up by the pair of them and they later made full admissions. They had done it before and because they asked for so little cash, in comparison to other blackmail attempts, they had been paid. They used the same method of operating, even taking into account the fact that they may be followed. This is why they stopped at the Irish Club after it had closed, the man had no intention of going in. It was just to continue the cover story if they should be caught. They understood being a courier would not attract the same punishment as being the main offenders. They were, however, sentenced as the main offenders and Kellogg's threw a party for our team. Unfortunately, those on the ground were unable to attend due to being on other live operations. There was no shortage of takers though and the guests were the office staff and non-combatants who always seem to bask in the glory of such successful operations.

Chapter Twenty-One

Back to Uniform with Stripes.

I HAD PASSED THE PROMOTION exam back in 1979 and, apart from an initial interview, I had not been on a promotion board. Towards the end of 1986, I decided it was about time and duly applied. The day before the interview, I travelled to Macclesfield and back with DS Frank Ball from the office. I had studied for the interview, but Frank pointed out that plans were afoot to turn the Regional Crime Squad into a National Crime Squad. I had not studied that. Frank was well up on it as he was trying for inspector and all the way there and back, he told me about it. The following day I went into the interview. There were one or two standard questions about finding your staff drunk or corrupt and then they went in depth into the proposed 'National Crime Squad'. What a lucky trip to Macclesfield that was. I passed with flying colours and just had to wait to be promoted.

'What's the farthest division from your house?' I had been called in from a local surveillance to take a phone call from the new DI who was at Chester Police Headquarters.

'I don't, know,' I replied, 'probably Macclesfield.'

'I thought as much,' he said in a conspiratorial voice. 'You've been promoted and that's where you're going, I haven't told you though; wait till you're told officially.'

I was to join Macclesfield Division in April 1987 as a uniformed sergeant. Frank was also promoted to inspector over the same period, and we shared a 'Leaving Do.'

Back into uniform, but this time as a sergeant. There are not many times when you can actually say, 'I am enjoying myself now.' You might be enjoying yourself, but it is only in retrospect that you can say, 'I really did enjoy that.' When going to Macclesfield, I could say, 'I am enjoying this.' I drew a uniform from the stores at Chester Headquarters and spent an afternoon pressing it. It was seven years since I had worn a uniform and even then, it was not for very long. I had enjoyed uniformed police work and I knew that I would enjoy it again. I also knew that, after a while, the novelty would wear off, and I would want to get back into plain clothes and do what I was best at. I had also spent the last two years as a scruffy plain-clothes officer on the RCS, a job almost totally alien to the normal life of an average police officer.

I started on nights with my block. I had taken over from a sergeant whose personality dictated that he would not be very well liked and who had been posted to the CID at Wilmslow. My joining the block was like a breath of fresh air. There was only one problem member really, a probationer who had not done well. He was a nice enough lad, but he did not seem to have the 'bearing' of a police officer. I was told that his last supervisors had written him up for being discharged as not having made the grade. I decided to make my own mind up and I did. I visited his landlady whilst he was working, and she expressed concern at the friends he was keeping. A short while later he was seen by a traffic patrol officer sitting alone in his car in the early hours of the morning. The car was parked in a remote picnic area. Something was amiss somewhere with regard to his personal life and, whilst on duty, he just couldn't hack it. I wrote up his report, with a recommendation that he would perhaps benefit from a job outside the force. This was taken up and he resigned. I am sure he has now made a success at something, but it would never have been police work.

Macclesfield is a strange place. There was a large mental hospital there called Parkside which, like most mental hospitals, had been redeveloped as a housing estate – leaving the mental patients to 'live in the community', and what a good idea that was! The joke in Macclesfield was that on Saturday nights, everyone on the streets had either been to Parkside, was going there or should be there. Either way, it was a fighting town, and we had our hands full. I started the practice of using a police van with darkened windows. I would put a few Bobbies in the back and carry out a form of zero tolerance policing. Anyone doing anything illegal, however minor, was spoken to, and arrested if need be. In the past, they had been used to giving V signs to panda cars and treating the police with contempt. That didn't happen on my block. The 'van' was now treated with the greatest of respect. Now, most towns have this form of police transport, and it is not unique any more. It was then and it certainly quietened Macclesfield down for a while.

One evening I was quietly sitting alone in a panda car in the main street at about 9.30pm, looking forward to going off at 10pm. It was quiet and peaceful.

'Are you busy?' I turned to see two rather attractive girls at the side of the car; they had been drinking but were not drunk.

'No, not really.'

'Fancy taking us on, we have always wanted a man in uniform?'

What do I say? What would most hot-blooded men say? Well dear reader, I didn't!

'Sorry girls, I would get the sack, not that I wouldn't like too.'

'Not even for these?' said the dark haired one, lifting her top and pressing two very attractive naked breasts through the driver's window.

Well, I still didn't! My social life was complicated enough as it was. I turned down what could have been a very pleasant end to my shift.

I had only been at Macclesfield for seven months when I was called in to see the chief inspector. I had an excellent block, inspector and fellow sergeants and we all got on well and did the job.

'You will have to go to work in Wilmslow, Paul; it will be nearer for you to travel.'

'I don't mind the travelling; I would rather stay here.' I replied.

'Well, there are too many junior sergeants here, so we will have to redress the balance and you were the last in.'

These were excuses and I knew it. What had I done wrong? I was to go to work in Knutsford for a while. But hang on… I knew Knutsford was a senior sergeant's post! He worked unsupervised with his own staff, so what's all this about junior sergeants? It was only later that I learnt that one of the 'senior sergeants' at Wilmslow had been playing away. His wife had found out and he had to be moved, so the real reason for my move was to enable a vacancy for him to be opened up at Macclesfield – and it was at my expense. That was the real reason for the move, I felt better about it anyway.

When I left Macclesfield, albeit that I had only been there a while, I got an emotional send off. I had enjoyed working with the block and the feeling appeared to be mutual. At the small leaving do, I was presented with a scroll that bore the words:

'This scroll is in honour of the following, **1633 Sergeant Paul Hurley.** *The below mentioned officers will remember with respect the comradeship he has shown.'* There was then a list of all eighteen block members. I was sorry to leave.

I went to Knutsford and loved it. I was my own boss and, although the town was quite posh, there was the usual yob trouble. Like nearly all Cheshire towns, an overspill council estate had been built to ensure that there was plenty of work for the police to do. On my staff, I had one PC with the nickname Salty Carter, a well-known character in the Cheshire Police, in fact one of the last. The force today is too antiseptic to entertain characters. There are many anecdotes involving Salty. On one occasion I was out with him when we came upon a group of kids at the side of the road. Salty leaned out of the window and they ran off. He was gone in a second, running after them, and I sat and waited. Fifteen minutes later, he returned with one of the lads, a very well spoken local. He had run off because he was out late and didn't want a home visit by the police.

After I told Salty to let him go, I asked where on earth he had been – he was covered from head to foot in sticky bobs!

'Sorry Sarge, I fell into a bush chasing them, the little bastards, but that's not all…'

'Go on,' I said, feigning resignation.

'I lost my radio in the bush!'

I then had to go and help him look for it; or rather I stood away from the bush and watched him getting covered in even more sticky bobs.

Although we worked alone, we were still technically on a block at Wilmslow; the block inspector was a nice, friendly, and extremely dapper man by the name of Stan Hilditch.

'Come on Paul, come and work here, I need you.'

'Thanks boss, but it's great at Knutsford, I went out picking mushrooms yesterday morning!'

Any other inspector would have said, 'Get your arse over here; you are being swapped with so and so.' Not Stan, he was too nice. Wilmslow police station was at that time still in the old building in Water Lane and was grossly overcrowded and not a very pleasant place to work. It was antiquated and cramped. There is now a modern police station in Hawthorn Street and the old one was, for a short time, a pub called The Blue Lamp before it was demolished.

I did move to work in Wilmslow after a while and almost immediately my appraisal was due. The chief inspector was a thoroughly nice man, but one famous for never saying what he meant. He would go all round it. 'Know what I mean, know what I mean, nudge-nudge, wink-wink, say no more, a nod's as good as a wink to a blind man.' That sort of thing. Stan did my appraisal, and I went to see the chief inspector for my interview. The appraisal or report on me was excellent; I couldn't have done better myself. Then we had a chat, or a chief inspector-type chat.

'Are you enjoying Wilmslow Paul?'

'Yes sir.'

'Girls nice here, are they?'

'Err, yes sir.'

'Nice as the ones in Knutsford, know what I mean, know what I mean?' he said, winking furiously.

'Yes sir, they are nice in both places.'

It went on like this for a while and afterwards I went and saw Stan.

'OK, was it?' he asked.

'Yeah, thanks for your report, it was great, he was a bit strange though.'

'What do you mean?' asked Stan.

'Kept going on about girls here and at Knutsford.'

Stan went red. 'Oh, sorry that will have been my fault, I told him that I wanted you to work here, and you didn't want to come.'

'Yes?'

'So, I told him you were probably shagging in Knutsford, I was only joking but he picked it up straight away,' Stan was looking very sheepish.

'Well thanks Stan, with friends like you, who needs enemies?' I said, but I was only joking; it was a pleasure to work with him. Again, I had a good block and we worked hard though looking back we were perhaps a bit heavy handed – one night I had to warn them to go easy as we were damaging too many prisoners. The damage was only caused using the minimum force, but it was still happening. Half an hour later I was dragging a lad up the street by his lapels after he had hit his girlfriend in front of me. The panda turned up and my warning to the block was repeated in a mimicking way.

'We will have to stop hurting people, isn't that right Sarge?'

'Alright, alright,' I had to agree though; there are times when you must take the gloves off. The police should be there to stop crime and arrest people, not be social workers in the way that they are becoming now. They should be feared and respected and never a figure of fun. Even now I cringe when I see idiots taking the mickey out of PCs and getting away with it.

We all have our pet hates and two of mine were the misuse of disability badges and cheeky parking – as a sergeant I didn't need to issue fixed penalty tickets, but I did keep some with me. I received cheers when I ticketed a Rolls-Royce parked in a bus stop in Wilmslow town centre. Disability badges are, I think, the most abused privileges issued today. I feel sorry for the people who genuinely need to use them, such as Brian Curzon with whom I was later to co-compile a local history book. Brian was so disabled that he had to drive seven miles to a village supermarket as he could then park immediately outside the door; he has since sadly died of his illness.

There are many complaints of people abusing disabled bays but, in the main, it is because far more people abuse disability badges. In towns and cities, the roads are clogged up with cars parked in no parking areas with badges in the windows. Wagons and busses find it difficult to get through. Once, when walking through Warrington, a car was parked in a dangerous place on a dangerous road on double yellow lines. Two Asians dressed all in white got out and strode healthily towards me. As they passed, I had to congratulate them on their rude health. They actually said, 'thank you!'

I only booked one car with a disabled badge though. He had parked in a narrow town centre road, the only car on that side whereas the other side would have been ok, and everything had to manoeuvre around him. He got a ticket for his trouble. I am breaking all the rules of political correctness here by being seen to criticise disability badges, but before you judge me Guardian reader go and stand for half an hour in a city street plagued by these badges and see how many genuinely need to be used. I won't mention electric invalid scooters with old men and enormous people in them driving proudly up the road with a stream of cars following them or hurtling dangerously through pedestrian shopping areas. And I won't ask 'what came first, the morbid obesity or the electric scooter that pushes you out of the way in Tesco?' Oops, I just did!

Chapter Twenty-Two

Dealing With Famous People

I WAS ON STATION SERGEANT duties one day in Wilmslow police station. The office was next door to the small control room with a through hatch. Control room staff were also responsible for dealing with callers at the desk.

'Can you come and have a look at this Sarge?' It was one of the officers in the control room. 'There are some people at the desk...'

I went out and, standing in the foyer, I saw two women and a man. The man was standing looking sheepish, and the women were shouting at each other. As I walked towards the desk, one of the women stormed out.

'What seems to be the trouble?' I asked.

'That woman has just rammed my car and this man is a witness,' said the remaining woman, indicating the still swinging front door.

What would appear to have happened was the woman at the desk had been looking for a parking space on the busy main street when she had seen the man start to pull away from the kerb. As he did so, she slotted in behind him. She then saw a car in which the other woman was sitting. It was in the centre of the road waiting for the man to move before taking his place. She had not seen it prior to 'stealing' the parking space. After the first woman had parked and got out, there was an altercation between them. The second woman then got into her car and reversed it violently into the side of the one by the kerb. There was another slanging match and all three came to the police station which was almost across the road. I had statements taken from both the woman at the desk and the man. There was a witness who had stood on the kerb watching but he was yet to be contacted.

I had been back in my office for a while when the officer shouted through, 'Phone call Sarge, its Mr Roache.'

'Mr Roache?' I queried.

'You know, Ken Barlow from Coronation Street, it was his wife who stormed off.'

I took the call and Bill Roache asked me if I needed to see his wife. I replied that I did, and he agreed to bring her in later that day. When he arrived, I took him into my small office. I was amazed at how short he was. It's hard to tell people's height from the TV. He asked me if I needed to interview his wife about a parking incident; she was sitting in the foyer.

'I'm afraid that we are not just talking about a motoring offence here,' I explained. 'Your wife would appear to have deliberately reversed into the other woman's car. Doing that is classed as criminal damage and is a crime.'

He explained that she had been through a traumatic time recently and this would do her no good at all. I sent an officer to get a statement off her and he came back to tell me that he did not think she had done it on purpose, despite what the other witnesses had said.

I got Sara and Bill Roache together and told them that there was an independent witness. I would contact him and if he said it could have been an accident, we could go down that route. I allowed her to leave without bailing her on the understanding that they returned when requested.

I now had to phone the other witness. 'Hello Mr Smith,' I said over the phone, 'Sergeant Hurley here from Wilmslow. I believe that you witnessed an accident in the town centre today.'

'An accident, an accident, I never saw any accidents, I saw one car deliberately reverse into another one, she rammed it on purpose dammit, accident my foot!' said the well-spoken independent witness in a voice that indicated he told people off on a daily basis.

'Well, what if the offending driver was not sure of the gears?' I said hopefully.

'Rubbish and bunkum, damn woman did it on purpose!'

I had got an independent witness who did not mince his words and he would make a statement to that effect.

Irrespective of the 'star' status, the PC was convinced that although she may have been irate, she did not intend to ram the other car. I got them back in and spoke with them together. I told Sara what the independent witness would say and pointed out that if she admitted criminal damage in the heat of the moment, she would probably be given a caution as it was her first offence. If she did not admit it, it would probably go to court. She explained to me again that the car, a Honda Accord, belonged to her husband. It was an automatic and she was not used to it. When the other woman stole the parking place that she was waiting for, she was mad and annoyed. But she forgot that the car was in reverse and stamped on the accelerator intending to drive off in disgust. Instead, the car lurched backwards. She had not done it on purpose and would never admit that she had been reckless, whatever the cost.

Although by then the use of admission statements under caution had fallen into disuse, being replaced by contemporaneous notes, I asked her if she would like to make one and leave the rest to me. This she did and I wrote it down. I then checked the car and noted the gears. She was reported for summons for driving without due care and attention and the couple left.

I prepared an advice file with a report saying that the car was an automatic and, with it in gear and a foot on the brake, it was easy to forget what gear it was in. I submitted it with a recommendation that it be dealt with as a motoring offence. It went to Inspector Terry White, my old sergeant, who did not agree with me. It was criminal damage, and she should be reported for it. The detective inspector did, likewise, stating that she should definitely be charged with criminal damage. It was then sent to the superintendent, Derek Lidster, my old DI at Northwich. He in turn made no comment but sent it to the Crown Prosecution Service for their advice. They agreed totally with me and recommended that Mrs Roache be summonsed for driving without due care and attention. She pleaded guilty to this less serious offence and received a few penalty points on her licence.

Irrespective of the occupation of those involved, there is still room for common sense to be considered and this is what I did. All parties in this altercation were respectable Wilmslow people, I believed her and would have treated anyone in the same way under identical circumstances. Sadly, Sara died suddenly at the young age of 58 some years later.

My idea of fair play and common sense came to the fore a short while later when I was again the station sergeant. A traffic officer brought in a man arrested on a breathalyser.

'I saw this man driving and he crossed the centre line on one occasion, so I followed him to his house. I obtained from him a breath test and it proved positive. I arrested him,' said the traffic officer in the officious way that most of them have.

The 'offender' was a middle-aged scientist. I sat him at the breathalyser machine and asked him what he'd had to drink. 'I have just had two pints, I only usually have one, but we won the match and the other team bought us another. I am very sorry; I know that you are only doing your job.' He said that he would probably lose his job now and appeared to me to be totally sober. He blew into the machine and was only about two points over the limit. I told him that he was only just over the limit and advised him that it may be in his own interest to have a blood test. He agreed and I waited a while before calling the police surgeon, thinking the delay may make him drop under the limit. When I paged the doctor, as fate would have it, he was just driving past the police station and came straight in. The man gave his blood test but was still slightly over the limit. He was banned from driving for a year as the law dictated and probably lost his job. I suggested to the zealous traffic man that perhaps his energies would be better expended doing something useful. I also suggested that he checked to see if I was on duty next time, he wished to persecute someone in that manner. Although they do a necessary job, I cannot help but think that without the traffic department, the police would have quite a good reputation with the general public.

Another breathalyser test I'll always remember was when an old farmer had crashed into a wall in Disley, a village that for some reason had remained in Cheshire on amalgamation, despite the need to pass through parts of Greater Manchester to get to it, or go across the hills the other way. He had provided a positive sample of breath and was taken to Macclesfield. At the police station, there was no substantive sergeant on duty, so he had to be brought to Wilmslow, a journey that took at least an hour in all. At Wilmslow, he stood in front of me, and, to all intents and purposes, he had never had a drink. He appeared stone cold sober. I booked him in and took him through to the machine. He blew in it and the result had me checking with the instruction manual.

'I am sorry,' I told him. 'This machine must be faulty. The figure you have just recorded indicates that you must now be in a coma and will probably die!'

'Eeee, no lad,' he replied, 'there's nowt wrong wi' thy machine, I drink a few bottles of whisky a day, it's about time tha' caught me, your lads have done me a favour.'

There was more chance of using common sense in those days than there is now. The police have become sanitised, politically correct and obsessed with doing everything by the book. Go against the rules now and the chance of getting the sack is very high. I was on duty one day when a policewoman came in to see me. She was very upset and told me that she had just bumped a panda car into the wall in the car park putting a big dent in it. Really, as per force orders, she should have been suspended from driving and after a suitable period re-tested before being allowed to drive police vehicles again. A total waste of manpower because of a momentary lapse. I made a phone call to a friendly garage and told her where to take the car for a crafty repair. She left and I had cause to pass the superintendent's office on the first floor. Derek Lidster was sat at his desk.

'Oh Paul,' he shouted.

'Yes boss.' I replied, stopping, and standing in the doorway. His window overlooked the car park.

'Bloody lucky I wasn't looking out of the window just now,' he smiled at me. 'I take it that any problems are being sorted?'

'Err, yes sir, nothing for you to worry about – as you know.'

'Thank you,' he replied, going back to his work as if nothing had happened. Unfortunately, in today's police force there is no room for bosses like Derek, or sergeants like me for that matter. The car was duly returned an hour later with no sign of damage and the policewoman lived to drive another day.

Although I had advanced police driving permit from my RCS course, I had never driven with blue lights flashing and two tones blaring. It is also fair to say that not all traffic officers were paid-up members of the Gestapo. One such was the traffic man attached to our block by the name of Dave. I enjoyed going out with him and he was, as were they all, excellent drivers. On one occasion we were behind a car that was obviously up to no good as it took off at high speed towards the motorway. We set off after it. Doing over 100 mph on a slightly twisty road is not so much scary as exhilarating and beats all white-knuckle rides. I was trying to control myself as I held the car phone and gave a commentary to the control room, shouting over the noise from the two tones. People who have enjoyed the scariest white-knuckle rides will know that you cannot help smiling manically. To do this and give a sensible and cool commentary is difficult. He had a start on us, and we passed under the Manchester airport runway underpass near to the Valley Lodge hotel well in excess of 100mph. Soon we reached the roundabout at the end to find the car we were chasing half way up a tree in the middle. Naturally the two occupants had jumped out and run away. Had it been an ordinary family in the accident they would almost certainly have been killed. It never seems to happen with teenage joy riders – they never wear seat belts and despite having the most horrendous accidents they seem in the main to walk (or run) away from them. We found one hiding near the roundabout and after a bit of persuasion by me he decided to tell us who his mate was. I arrested him and we took him to the police station. The station sergeant on duty was a rather an insipid man (the reason why Stan wanted me there) who would never recognise a cut corner or a bit of the Ways and Means Act. He was purely by the book.

'Those marks on your face, were they caused by the accident?' he asked innocently.

The lad started to speak and then quickly changed what he was going to say to 'Err, yes.'

I looked down and Dave had inadvertently trodden on his foot!

My forte for the plain-clothes side of police work was soon discovered and I was nominated to set up a plain-clothes department at Wilmslow. One of my staff was to be the then chief constable David Graham's daughter, Morag Arterton, probably one of the best natural thief takers I have ever worked with. A good example of this was one day when we were driving in a panda car through the car park of the Valley Lodge hotel one evening. It was quite full and as we passed two men getting into a Toyota 3 litre Supra. Morag shouted to me that they were wearing trainers – and this was not somewhere people came to in the evening wearing trainers. I stopped the car and got out. As I did, they jumped into the Supra and roared off. Morag was driving and we took off after them, a 1600cc Vauxhall Astra panda car versus a 3000cc sports car, no competition really and despite Morag's best and very scary efforts they escaped. The Supra had been stolen in Manchester and they were about to steal another from the car park when we intervened.

Just before Christmas 1988, I had planned a party at home for colleagues, friends, and family; it was to be quite a big do and the night before I got a phone call from Alan Brocklehurst telling me that one of the guests, my good friend Neil Gibson, had died in a road accident. Neil had been one of our small team of DCs in the Winsford CID. As a result, the prospective police invites to the party would not be coming but as there were a lot of family members attending, I couldn't really put it off. The news was a shock; Neil had been promoted to detective sergeant and had been on the Serious Crime Squad. He had been returning from an operation when his car left the road, crashed through a hedge and he was killed. As a result of this, there was to be a move around. Brocky was to get his job and I was to return to the RCS in his place as a detective sergeant.

Chapter Twenty-Three

Back To the RCS & Domestic Upheaval

I HAD ENJOYED MYSELF in uniform, and later plain clothes, but the novelty of ordinary police work was starting to wear off and so in January 1989, I was happy to return to the Runcorn branch office of the Regional Crime Squad. My partner this time was a DC who was in his late thirties and single. He was a big drinker and a big gambler, still living at home in Warrington with his parents. I suppose he could be described as macho where women were concerned. He was a man who thought that they belonged in the bed or the kitchen. My old mate Paul was still in the office and there were some new faces. I had only been there for a short time when thankfully a new DCI arrived to replace Brezhnev in the form of DCI Dave Holt, my old DI from Northwich, and a man who did not suffer fools easily. DS John Phoenix, another ex-Northwich mate, was also in the office. The secondment started off with a quiet period with mundane surveillances and the like.

Later that year, in the October, I left the marital home. Things had not been right for a long time, in fact probably since I got married. Brenda is a very nice woman and we had always got on quite well. I had never been the perfect husband and, if the truth were known, we were not exactly made for each other. When you marry young, you can settle into a rut and stay there forever. She was an excellent mother to Mark, Andrea, Paul and Victoria and a good wife in a lot of ways. We had been married for 20 years and had brought up four children. Well, really, she had brought up four children; I was either away in the Navy, or away in the police. This was not enough for me, nor was it enough for her and we had both looked elsewhere for companionship. In my case, I met Rose. A fantastic person and a girl that I did and still do get on well with in every possible way; we have everything in common. She is younger than me by eleven years and when I met her she was a clerical officer with the gas board. I persuaded her to take up the gas board's offer to re-train as a computer systems analyst and this she did. We are total soul mates.

I left home after a lot of consideration to live with her in her nearby house. I decided that I had to make the split as amicable and painless as possible for the children. Brenda was like most wives in the same situation, vindictive and nasty. I didn't react and I took everything she threw at me. I carried on looking after the financial side and ensured that any damage was minimal. We had the same solicitor and fortunately I had bought the house in 1985 for £28,000 and carried out a lot of work on it myself; when I came to sell it in 1989, I got £74,000 for it. So, after paying off the mortgage, there was enough money to buy Brenda a house with a small mortgage; I took very little for myself.

The children got on well with Rose, although Andrea had all the airs and graces of a typical pro-mum seventeen-year-old girl. She didn't like Rose at all and naively blamed everything on her. She certainly made her feelings known. Soon after Andrea joined the Wrens and went on to serve on the Ark Royal in the Adriatic, one of the first women to serve at sea and one of the last members of the Wrens before women were incorporated into the Navy proper. She had her moment of fame when a national television documentary was filmed on the aircraft carrier Ark Royal. and was asked if it was right for women to serve on ships. The interviewer then went along the line asking the girls various questions before coming to Andrea who said that the men called them split arses. When asked what that meant she said probably because they wore split skirts. When asked to comment again she explained that it wasn't becaue they wore split skirts, so what was it she was asked to which she replied, well we are, 'split arses'.

Nothing was cut and I made sure that I taped the programme, it can still be seen on Utube, she is now a highly respected paramedic with a son.

Once the dust from my marriage split had settled, I think that, as far as is possible, I did the best for all concerned. We got divorced and I have remained friends with Brenda, well, as friendly as is possible under the circumstances. Andrea and Rose are now best mates, so things come together eventually.

Unbeknown to me at the time, I was about to be nominated as the next North West undercover operative by Dave Holt. Unfortunately, though, because I had left the family home and, for a while, my domestic life was in a mess, this spoilt my chance of the undercover job. The job is stressful enough in itself and the partners of undercover operatives must be vetted in order to ensure that they are suitable. The duties would entail long periods away from home and, in a lot of cases, involve being incommunicado. The relationship had to be on the firmest and most trustworthy of footings – and a new relationship could never be that – so unfortunately anyone going through a period of domestic upset cannot even be considered. I was disappointed, as I would have enjoyed the challenge. Had I got that job, I would have gone through intensive training with the army and spent most of my time undercover, probably down south. Que sera, sera, though I'm sure I would have loved it.

Now let's have a few snippets of routine RCS work.

'I want all the sergeants in my office now!' boomed the voice from the DCI's office. It sounded like Dave Holt had something important to say and it soon transpired that he did. Some time earlier an eighteen-year-old estate agent by the name of Julie Dart had been kidnapped and later murdered. A letter that the kidnapper had written had been passed to the Runcorn RCS office. In it, he stated that he was now threatening to derail an express train on the West Coast Main Line. The letter was in a polythene sleeve, and we read it: it was a blackmail demand. If the rail authorities did not pay up, then the act would take place. I pointed out, remembering my train spotting days, that there were parts of the letter that made it obvious this person knew something about the rail infrastructure. The letter was dispatched to the forensic science laboratory by motorcycle. The blackmailer, who we later discovered was named Michael Sams, wanted the police to act as a go between and insisted his contact was to be a policewoman. A trained female undercover officer from down south was chosen for this task, and I think that on two occasions she was to be at the phone boxes on the platform at Crewe Station to await a call. I was one of the footmen on the station covering her, but there was no call, or if there was, she did not get it.

His next move was uncovered when a stone with the home address of a British Rail executive chalked on it was found at the side of the track in Staffordshire. This had been hung from the overhead gantry with the intention of smashing through the driver's window of the next locomotive. Thankfully it had been unsuccessful. His second kidnap victim, estate agent Stephanie Slater was later released unharmed. When he was arrested, it transpired that Sams lived near the railway and was, as I had deduced, a train enthusiast. After Leslie Whittle had been kidnapped by Donald Neilson and imprisoned in a drain near Cannock Chase in 1975, there were many mistakes and as a result she died. It was decided that all kidnap offences be dealt with by The Regional Crime Squad. We were especially trained and had to take part in a Pivot Peripheral course to learn the techniques allowed to safely carry out such a duty. I don't intend to say anymore about this.

We did a static observation during the period when an undercover man was setting up the arrest of some criminals for lorry thefts. The plan was to strike when they started unloading the vehicle. I was out on foot watching the premises, and I had a pickaxe handle behind my back. I gave the order to strike. Thinking that the cars would all roar up at any second, like they do on the telly, I calmly walked down a slope to where the gangsters and the undercover man were talking. I was getting closer to them with no sign of back-up, and soon I reached them. They looked at me quizzically and one asked me what I wanted. Shit, I thought, I'm standing amongst a group of lorry thieves on my own with a pickaxe handle behind my back. I can't really start discussing football, can I, so what do I do now? The factory unit was miles away from any other signs of habitation, at the far end of an industrial estate, and it was the evening, I had absolutely no reason to be there and if they saw the pickaxe handle, they would not offer me a cup of tea.

I was about to give up and run like hell when there was the screech of tyres – the 'well prepared' surveillance team had finally put down their pies and newspapers and found the lock-up and, in the nick of time, come to my assistance. The men started to run, pursued by the troops. Chris Caswell my partner, managed to pick on the undercover man to chase, catch and thump. The job ended well, all the thieves were arrested, and the property recovered.

It was time for Paul Sinclair, my ex-partner, to leave the squad and return to the Merseyside Police. His do was to be in the Cricket Club at Runcorn and we planned behind his back to get a stripogram. There was concern that Paul being as shy as he was the plan may fall flat, as he would run off or something. It was a worry, but the plan went ahead. This was my first real experience of a proper double bluff!

Everyone was merrily drunk when the girl arrived in her fishnet tights, schoolgirl clothes and straw boater.

She started her speech. 'For all of your misbehaving on the squad Paul, you need disciplining.' Everyone laughed and looked at Paul, who didn't seem too bothered. She continued.

'So, Paul *Hurley*, come out here.' I was stunned and the place was in uproar – it seemed that everyone knew but me. I meekly went out and was stripped down to my pants. When it is your leaving do, you have to expect that this sort of thing may happen and you dress accordingly, and you wear clean designer underpants. Sadly, this was not the case here: I had ordinary tatty baggy ones on. I was told to bend over, and I did, expecting a little tickle with the whip that she had. It was not to be that easy. She drew it back and three times it made a loud cracking sound before ripping into my back, and after this I had to make her stop. My back was covered in wheals. They were so bad that I demanded pints all night from the people who wanted to have a look. Rose was coming to pick me up and when she did, someone told her that when I was made to lift my leg up in front of Mary, the office secretary, my willy fell out. I got my first new relationship telling off. The reason they had double bluffed was because they knew that Paul would probably have been too embarrassed to allow the show to go ahead – but that I was daft enough to!

Chapter Twenty-Four

Stolen Porsches, a Kidnapped Child & National News

DON'T YOU JUST LOVE IT when things just fall into place without even trying? It was late 1989 when Richard Woolley, a Wilmslow officer, had asked my advice on a job and as a result we had both gone to Bangor in Northern Ireland to investigate. There is another side to this story, with a wonderful piece of timing, as I had for some time been trying to arrest a wanted man in Blackpool. I had set up observations on a house that he was believed to visit and, although he was seen on one occasion, he had made off in a car. Despite me ramming him in the squad car he still escaped. Whilst we were in Bangor, I received a phone call from our Blackpool contact to say where he was in Blackpool. I then liaised with the local CID and after a long chase he was caught by local officers. We then got on with our Northern Ireland inquiry. It was a success, although I can't really remember much about it now, but suffice to say that when Richard was contacted by a friend in the Greater Manchester police asking for a good contact in the RCS, he recommended me. I worked alone as I liked to do and visited an officer called Steve Mann from the No 1 TASS Traffic Area Support Services group in Manchester. This is a squad of officers who specialise in car crime and drive high-powered plain cars. The squad was later immortalised when they were subject of a fly-on-the-wall TV documentary series. Steve was the main character in this programme and later attended my wedding to Rose

There had been a spate of thefts of Porsches in the North West and Steve suspected a certain team from Manchester were the culprits. I worked on it with him; the stolen cars were all quite new and expensive. Although I had a partner, I worked either alone or with non-RCS personnel at the start of that particular inquiry. We had a good informant providing us with information which meant, unlike other operations, surveillance was not the vehicle for evidence gathering. The main work, though, was to start after the arrests.

We executed a search warrant on the home of the main offender and recovered a large quantity of parts from Porsches. The car parts were taken to the Greater Manchester Police vehicle pound, where they took up a considerable amount of space. In all, we arrested three people and interviewed them at length.

A relationship was built up both prior to the arrest, during interview and later when they were bailed. They told us about all the Porsches they had taken, and it amounted to nearly 20 – most of them quite new. The main man, Paul Gort was a genuine Porsche fanatic. He was obsessed with that make of car and there was nothing he didn't know about them. Show him any nut or screw and he could say exactly where it had come from. The team had several ways of taking the cars, the main one being with the use of a scissor blade.

When I told a representative from Porsche UK that their cars were being stolen with a scissor blade, they would not believe it. It must be kept in context though as Porsches have excellent security systems. Their owners, however, are usually quite well to do and live in houses that reflect this. If the house is set in its own grounds, there is a tendency to leave the car unlocked. The team would follow a quality Porsche and see where it was parked, then return later and steal it using the scissor blade, or go on to another if it had been secured properly. They travelled the country in search of the easily stolen cars, including the City of London. Later they were assisted by technology that could be operated near to a person who was using their vehicle's remote central locking and alarm system. This instrument would then 'steal' and input the digital security combination into its own memory bank. The thieves could then use it to unlock, hotwire and steal the car.

Each stolen car was then driven to a garage in Manchester and stripped down to its shell. The interior and all movable parts, such as the doors, windows, and fittings, would be removed and taken to the handlers of them. The body shell would then go to the scrap yard, or simply taken up onto the moors and dumped. The parts that we seized and stored at the police pound had a value of three quarters of a million pounds (in 1989), which gives some insight into the values involved. The thieves, however, saw nothing like this amount even though each one was worth between £40,000 and £80,000 back in 1989.

One of the handlers that we knew of before the arrests was involved in Porsche racing and had farm premises in Northwich, Cheshire. I will call him Lewis. It was here that I learnt another lesson about trust. Directly opposite his premises was a pub, The Slow and Easy, and my old partner DS Phil Bowyer used it. I told Phil of the operation and that we would really like to get an observation point overlooking the farm.

'The landlord here is sound as a pound,' said Phil, 'he'll let you use the front window upstairs.'

With this, I pulled the landlord to one side. 'What's the chance of using your front room to watch the farm opposite?' I asked.

'No problem, I always like to help you lads, big mate of mine Phil!' he replied in a conspiratorial manner. I arranged to contact him later.

But I was not to get the opportunity as I received a phone call at home from the informant. 'What's going on? Lewis knows he's being watched, some bastard's grassed.'

It was only one day since I had approached the landlord and my informant was telling me that the operation had been rumbled.

I shot back to the pub and hammered on the door. 'Why have you told Lewis that we intended watching him?' I said angrily to the licensee. He looked totally shocked.

'I haven't honestly, I wouldn't do that.'

I could tell that he was lying and sarcastically thanked him for his help. I made sure that I contacted a friend on the brewery management and told him of the 'assistance' that one of his landlords had given me.

Fortunately, and unexpectedly, this did not deter 'Lewis' from continuing with his nefarious business. When we later searched the farm, with the assistance of the offenders, we recovered quite a few stolen parts. Although he was a respected member of the saloon car racing fraternity and the owner of a Porsche racing team, he appeared at Chester Crown Court and received an eighteen-month prison sentence. The enquiries went on and we kept in touch with the main offender, Paul, who later, whilst on bail, resumed his thieving activities. We caught him again as we had an informant informing on the informant!

The operation had virtually wound down and we were waiting to go to court. It was late 1989 and I was sitting at home watching the TV news. The Berlin Wall was starting to look a little shaky after the momentous changes in the Soviet Union, but the main national news report was the story of the kidnapping of a young girl in Manchester. She had been in the school playground in Cheadle Hume with other children when a black car had drawn up containing two masked men and she had been forced, screaming, into the back and driven away. It was a very brutal and high-profile kidnapping, but it was just news to me, and I thought nothing more of it. The following day it made the headlines in the national daily newspapers.

I was in the office when I got a phone call from a senior officer in the Greater Manchester police. 'I'm told that you know Paul Gort quite well?' I confirmed that he was a registered informant of mine and asked him what the problem was.

'That kidnap yesterday, it was Paul Gorts daughter, and we believe he was behind it.'

I agreed to help them in any way I could, and he arranged with my DCI for me to go over and work with them on it. Having spoken with the detective inspector in charge

George Garden and it was agreed that I would have a free hand. After the kidnapping, a letter had been received from Paul stating that he had taken his daughter abroad. The letter was postmarked France. He was not coming back.

I went to Paul's family home to find a large contingent of local and national television and press reporters outside. My relationship with his parents was a good one and they said they believed he was still in France. He was going to phone them at a given time that day. I was aware that Paul had not been at all happy with the way his daughter Emma had been dealt with by the Social Services. She she was born to his girlfriend when she was 14 years old and had been immediately put into care and then to foster parents, Mr and Mrs Hyde and they were not allowed access to her. He had an axe to grind and, to be honest, if what he said was true, he had quite a reasonable case. He had, however, taken the law into his own hands.

DI Gardner, the officer in charge of the operation had given me total responsibility to do as I saw fit and I decided to go out to talk to the press. I told them that I was expecting a phone call and I asked them if they could wait away from the front of the house.

I approached the Daily Mirror reporter and put to him the idea that he could have sole rights to the story, in exchange for highlighting Paul's' grievances. He jumped at the chance.

The phone rang. 'Paul, it's Paul Hurley, come back now, the Daily Mirror have agreed to interview you and print your side. You were a prick doing this, but it could all come out alright, what do you say?' I spoke with him for a little longer and he replied.

'I don't know, I will have to think about it and ring you back.'

'Well hurry up, I will only have this freedom for a short while and after that you will be in deep shit.' I remained at the house and time was getting on. I was being given a lot of freedom and didn't want to let everyone down. The detective inspector was phoning me periodically and I knew he would soon be getting impatient and wondering if I should have had such a free hand.

The afternoon came and Paul phoned back. 'I don't know Paul; I just don't know what to do.' We had a short chat, but I was not happy that he was going to come back. His brother and friend were in the house, and they had denied any involvement, stating that they believed that he was in France. 'Get in the car you two,' I ordered them. They did, and we went for drive, I did consider the fact that members of the press would follow us.

'You are a pair of lying bastards and you are not doing Paul any favours,' I told them. They continued to deny any knowledge. I told them that the offer to put his side of it in the national press would run out very soon: today it was interesting, tomorrow it would not be. I went on and on at them and eventually, after nearly an hour of being put under the most extreme pressure, they cracked.

His brother was the first. 'Will he be in the shit?'

My foot was in the door, so to speak, and it could only get better. 'You know I will do my best, is he in England?'

'Yes,' he replied, 'not far from here.'

'Come on, let's go,' I said. 'Direct me.'

We drove to a house in the Manchester suburb of Blackley. I went round to the back and the door was unlocked. I walked in and through to the front room. It was sparsely furnished with a television in the corner. On the television the news was on and there was a home movie of Paul's daughter Emma walking down a path, smiling at the camera. It was followed by an appeal for her safe return, given by her foster parents and senior officers from Greater Manchester Police. Sitting watching were Paul, his girlfriend, and Emma. There was no need for words. I looked at Paul and he looked at me in a manner that said he was beaten.

'Who told you?' was all he said. I did not answer. I phoned the inspector and told him: he was over the moon. I asked him if he could wait 20 minutes and then come and collect them. I then phoned the Daily Mirror and invited them to attend. They did but were beaten to it by some of the waiting press corps, who had probably followed me for the past hour. I locked the back door and with the front door in view, waited at the top of the stairs while Paul was given the opportunity to talk to them. Twenty minutes later the detective inspector turned up and was filmed and photographed leaving the house with the little girl in his arms. At Ashton-under-Lyne police station that night, I was introduced to the foster parents as the officer who recovered the young girl. They were extremely happy and hugged me. Paul and his girlfriend spent the night in the cells.

The recovery of the girl made the national news that night, but the following day the Berlin wall was breached, and the story was relegated to the inside pages. Paul went to Knutsford Crown Court and was remanded in custody. I bought all the national papers with his story in and gave them to him in his cell. I asked him about the letters that had been written by him and sent from France. He explained that they had been written in advance and taken over by the men who he paid to do the job. A short time later he appeared at Knutsford Crown Court for both the cars and the kidnapping and went to prison.

I recommended Steve for a commendation for his part in catching the Porsche thieves, but he only got a letter of thanks. The detective inspector, DI Gardner however, recommended that I be commended for both jobs and some time later I learned that I was to be commended by the chief constable of Greater Manchester Police, James Anderton. The ceremony was at the Force Training Centre in Manchester, and I took along Rose; I was in my best suit and driving my Honda Accord. The car was my pride and joy and I had owned it for six years. I received an illuminated framed commendation – very nice, I thought. My last chief constable's commendation from Cheshire had been sent to me in a brown envelope! Afterwards there was a buffet and then we left to travel home. On the way, we were driving down Princess Parkway and it was the rush hour. We decided to pull in at the Princess Hotel for a drink and for the traffic to ease a little. As the lights changed a car flashed me through and I drove forward. I then discovered that it was a dual carriageway and a car travelling up the nearside lane slammed into me. It was the end of a very pleasant day. Luckily no one was hurt, but I had written off my pride and joy!

Chapter Twenty-Five

Crafty old blokes and Hide & Seek

BACK TO THE CUT AND THRUST of detective work…

'Hello, Paul, there's vodka being punted around the pubs in Liverpool for £27 a gallon, it's a regular delivery run.' I was at home having my tea when 'Billy' phoned.

'Sounds good, who's doing it?' I asked.

'Some old codgers from Belle Vale.'

Well, that's unusual, I thought, there seems to be an upper age limit for scally-type jobs like that one and most of the offenders are young bucks. Maybe they were part of one of the gangster teams so beloved in Liverpool. Either way, I would have a look at it.

'I swear by almighty God that the evidence I shall give will be the truth, the whole truth and nothing but the truth.' I was in the home of a Liverpool magistrate, and I had taken my Bible with me to swear on. 'I have received good information, sir, that at this particular address in Belle Vale, there is a large supply of vodka which is being sold in the pubs.' I always thought it strange, swearing on bibles in people's front rooms, but that was how search warrants had to be done.

'Has the source been reliable before?' he asked.

'Yes sir, on quite a few occasions,' I replied truthfully, although there were times when magistrates were given a story with a modicum of poetic license to ensure a 'wing and a prayer' fishing expedition search could be carried out. The warrant supplied to me was signed and I had my 'ticket.'

The following morning, I took a team to the address – a small, terraced council house, not far from the police station in Belle Vale. The door was opened by a small man in his mid fifties, who allowed us in; it didn't really matter whether he did or not really, we were going in anyway. We searched the house – nothing. 'Billy' has let me down, I thought, and the lads with me were not too happy. On the way out, I saw that the bin cupboard in the small porch was locked.

'What's in there?' I asked.

'Just the bin, boss,' he replied.

'Well get the key and we'll look,' I instructed him.

'Err, I don't know where it is,' he replied sheepishly.

After being assured that the cupboard door would soon come off if he didn't hurry up, the missing key was produced. Bingo. The small shed was filled from floor to ceiling with empty plastic gallon containers and a few large carboys filled with some sort of spirit. He was locked up and the containers and other items seized.

It transpired that this man and his accomplice, who was also later arrested, worked for a local bottling company, Halewood Vintners. They had devised a crafty scam to make money (now that is an unusual occurrence in deep, dark Liverpool!). Vodka is simply diluted ethanol. It comes into the country in its pure state in large road tankers before being pumped into massive stainless-steel containers at the depot. Prior to bottling it is mixed with about two-thirds purified water; a chemical 'fingerprint' is added to enable later checks to be made into its origin. After perhaps a few other cosmetic additives, it is bottled, duty is added, and it is sold as vodka.

What these crafty old sods had discovered was that the ethanol was pumped from the road tanker to the vats by means of a large-diameter hosepipe, bigger than a fireman's hose, about 20 foot long. When the vat was full, they carefully disconnected it at both ends and held the hose up so that the ethanol that was still in the hosepipe did not pour away, and they could fill about two large carboys with its contents. As the stuff, prior to tax duty, only cost 10 to 20 pence per gallon, there was no need for the company to bother about this amount of waste that should have been washed away.

They would then take the ethanol home where they had bought job lots of gallon containers. These were filled with two-thirds council house tap water and one-third ethanol. They then had a regular run delivering it to pubs in the city centre. These unscrupulous pubs would pay them £27 per gallon for the stuff and decant it into branded vodka bottles. Well, that was the job done; now to get the evidence. In the meantime, the two men were bailed. They had told me what they had done but would not name the pubs they had been supplying.

I visited the distilling company. 'We'll deal with them, but as for making a complaint, how can we? The stuff was just waste.'

I was up against my first hurdle: the firm did not want to make a complaint and why should they? They had not lost anything. I travelled down to Bicester in Oxfordshire to speak with the ethanol importers, of which there were very few. Apart from a statement outlining the method of importation and where it came from, they could not help either. The pubs using it would have committed the only substantive offence that I could come up with, and I didn't know who they were. So, the crafty old sods got away with it. At least the scam was ended as the company took steps to see that in future the waste was washed away. My main lesson was an insight into the vast amount of money the government makes in alcohol duty. I still managed though to get a few bob for 'Billy' in return for the information.

On occasions, we would carry out surveillance by using a tracker. If we were able to fit a tracking device to a bandit car, either with the help of a hire company, or by sticking a limpet underneath, we could follow it at a safer distance in a 'tracker vehicle' – one that is fitted with a device to receive directions from the offender's bugged car. We could follow from quite a way back, with the surveillance cars following ready to take over if anything went wrong, which it frequently did. This was by no means a foolproof way to follow someone and 'losses' happened quite frequently. On a road running parallel for instance, the team could be committed to the wrong road before they realised and would have a hard job to get back on to the right one. Where the bandit car took a slip road for instance out of visual contact with the tracker vehicle.

On one occasion, the 'tracker' became unserviceable in Stockport, and I had to rush back to Runcorn, a distance of about thirty-five miles along the M56, to get a replacement. My partner for the day was a policewoman from the Manchester RCS office and we took off at top speed, collected a new tracker vehicle – a beige Vauxhall Cavalier estate – and set off back. By now it was dark, and I was doing 125 miles per hour in the outside lane of the motorway when I saw the flashing lights in the distance behind me.

'Shit,' I said, 'this is all we need.' I slowed down and pulled over to the hard shoulder. The Traffic Range Rover stopped behind me and I got out and walked back. Both officers were still in the Range Rover, and I walked to the driver's side.

'Police, mate,' I said, my face level with his, 'I've got to get to Stockport urgently. We're on a live surveillance.'

He ignored me. His face was no more than a foot from mine, and he was looking at me, but he ignored me.

'Come on, can I get going?' I said urgently looking into the inscrutable face of a man who appeared unbelievably ignorant. He was looking straight at me and completely ignoring me. Then I had the answer! He calmly pressed the button to lower the electric window. With the lights from the motorway, I couldn't see that it was shut and didn't know that the ignorant smart-arse could not hear me.

'Do you know how fast you were going then?' he asked sneeringly.

'Yes, about 120,' I replied. 'It's a police car, can I go now?'

'I heard nothing from the control room about cars doing that speed, why didn't you tell them?'

'We're on a covert operation and don't advertise the fact,' I said, becoming rather annoyed, anyway you could have checked the blocked registration plate.

'Didn't you see us behind you?' he said, not giving up easily.

'When you are doing 120, you don't feel the need to check your mirrors very often,' I said with a hint of sarcasm. 'Now Constable, can I go?' Why couldn't these cowboys stick to persecuting motorists, making people drive slowly and escorting heavy loads? Perhaps a little unfair, I suppose.

'Let the control room know in future,' he said, dismissing me like a naughty schoolboy, and we continued on our way.

Chapter Twenty-Six

Chasing the Welsh Nationalists

LIFE GOES ON IN THE SLEEPY world of the Regional Crime Squad and another time in the early 1990s an operation in Wales involved watching the movements of a team of Welsh Nationalists who we believed were planning to blow up a pipeline. We followed them for a while and recorded their movements. Although many IRA men have, over the years, been arrested, the same cannot be said for the Welsh Nationalists. There had been very little success in investigating them.

We saw them off on the ferry at Holyhead when they went to take part in a Sinn Fein march in Ireland and when they returned, we continued to watch them. We had been billeted in the halls of residence at Bangor University and when off duty enjoyed the 'night life' of one of the smallest cities in Britain. After midnight, two of the Welsh officers went to the suspect vehicle, which was parked in a council estate. It was their job to affix the tracker device underneath the car ready for the morning when the surveillance would start. Unfortunately, at the same time, one of the neighbours decided to visit the toilet and look out of his window.

The following morning, we were all set; the location was the small Welsh town of Llangefni on the island of Anglesey. Suddenly the radio burst into life from the tracker vehicle.

'There's movement on the target vehicle – stand by.' We all started the cars ready for the off.

'It's off, off, off, up the high street towards Bangor.' We were ready.

'No, wait, it's done a 'recipe' (turned around) and is travelling back. It's now a stop, stop, stop, and wait, it's going round in circles.' It then went quiet for a while and the next voice was that of the detective inspector in charge.

'Stand down, back to Bangor University.'

On arrival, we found that the targets had been told that someone had been tampering with the car and they had found the device. They had taken it straight to their solicitor who was demanding an explanation from the North Wales Police. I offered to take my partner and go and 'steal' the tracker back from the solicitor, but the offer was declined. We drove back to Runcorn, and it was left to the chief constable of North Wales to deny all knowledge of the operation. A press release issued later would go on to explain that the device was actually a listening device used for intelligence gathering! Rather that than admit that the team were subject of a surveillance operation.

On the way home that night, with Terry Oates, we lived close to each other so shared lifts, we stopped as usual for a drink at the Leigh Arms pub at Acton Bridge. The landlord, Trevor, was a good friend and born-and-bred Welsh. As I stood at the bar with Terry, he grabbed me from behind and said jokingly:

'What have you been sticking on our cars then?'

'What do you mean?' I asked, feigning innocence.

'You know what I mean, I've just seen it on the TV news and I knew straight away that it was you lot.' We had a laugh but admitted nothing.

The set-up on the RCS was changed and instead of one sergeant and one constable working together as a team, the sergeant was given a team of three. This made two teams, one consisting of two constables and the other consisting of the sergeant and the third constable. I was now working with DC Jane Barnard, the only woman in the office. One of the first jobs that I did with Jane involved a man who ingratiated himself into the company of lonely single women, started a relationship and then emptied their bank accounts. It did not really fit the criteria for an RCS job, but because he now lived in the village of Stock Cross in Hampshire, we were allowed to do it as it was an Ellesmere Port job. Jane and officers from Ellesmere Port did the background work and dealt with some of the women he had taken for a ride. Apparently, they had all been 'in love' with him and did not see what he was up to until it was too late. When the initial enquiries were completed, it was left to us to arrest him. We set off in a hire car for Southampton, with me driving. Jane promised to drive back. On the way, we passed the suspect's house and familiarised ourselves with its location, ready for an early morning call the following day. After meeting our contact at Southampton police station, we were shown to our hotel. 'If you want a drink later,' he said, 'You can go to the police club around the corner, only go sooner rather than later as some of the local CID lads go there early doors. After that it becomes the Blue Rinse club.'

'What do you mean?' I asked, never having heard the term before.

'You'll see if you stay,' he replied. 'It has been taken over by the police pensioners and they run it like an old people's home, you know, music turned down and all that.'

We had our dinner in the hotel and decided to follow his advice and go for an early drink in the police club. At the door, there was a combination lock, and we were pressing it without success when a local PC joined us.

'It's OK, I'll do it, where are you from?' We told him and he opened the door and led us in to the large bar area which had a small dance floor. He insisted on getting the first round. I had a pint; Jane had a short and he had a coke. We told him what we were there for and then he started to tell us what he did.

'I am the stolen vehicle officer. There's nothing I don't know about cars, I'll have another Coke, thanks.' He was a professional bore, drone, drone, logbooks, drone, engine numbers, and more drone.

Then 'I'll have another Coke,' drone. At one stage, Jane went to the toilet.

'What are you still doing with the boring sod?' she said when she returned.

The place was filling up with pensioners and their partners; the music was constantly being turned down after repeated complaints until it could not be heard. Games of dominoes were being played and sweet sherries ordered. The place really did resemble an old people's home occupied by self-righteous pensioners who 'had done their bit' and now were enjoying the fruits of their labour. Unfortunately, this was at the expense of the people who were still labouring and who would put money in the till in far greater amounts than the old half-pinters who had commandeered the place! The local CID lads had left after one drink and our boring companion was still droning on – then a new barmaid came on duty.

'It's my round,' said our friend. 'A pint, a vodka and orange and a Coke please.'

'He's not having that Coke!' said the new barmaid, indicating our friend. You are having something stronger.'

'No,' he pleaded. 'You know I'm trying to keep off the booze.'

'You are having your usual and no arguments.' The Coke was deleted from the order and replaced with strong lager.

Two rounds later, our boring new friend had before our eyes stopped being an ugly duckling and blossomed into a swan: he was really a thoroughbred party animal and lounge lizard. Gone was the talk of work, gone was the drone, drone and in came flirting with the barmaids, telling mucky jokes and telling the old blokes to shut up. He was transformed!

'Right, we're off,' he declared, in a manner that said the decision has been made. 'Come on, I'll stop off on the way and get changed.' We went out to his car and piled in. After a short drive, he stopped and left us in the car for about five minutes, returning in his best disco gear complete with medallion. Off we went again and into a nightclub. He was welcomed with open arms by the bouncers and staff, obviously a regular, and we were not allowed to buy a drink as his friends saw to it. The local CID had arrived as well, obviously to escape the pensioners.

At 2am, I was starting to fall by the wayside and had three full pints beside me when he declared that we would be moving on, this time it was to a casino over the road. Jane frequented casinos, so knew her way around and we had a few bets – well at least I think we did. At 4.30am, still full of life, he dropped us off at our hotel.

Two-and-a-half hours later we were up and off to arrest our man. After this was successfully carried out, we set off with Jane driving but after a few miles it was apparent that she was still suffering the after-affects of meeting our new friend. I offered to drive, and she didn't need asking twice. She promptly went to sleep in the passenger seat for the five-hour journey back to Ellesmere Port. Our prisoner was handed over to the CID at Ellesmere Port and we went off duty, in my case to sleep.

It should be remembered that in a lot of cases the RCS is there to do the following, the watching and the arresting. Usually that is where our involvement ends as we hand over the prisoners for someone else to do the paperwork. This is not always the case, but it is when straight arresting is required, and I like to think that I got quite good at finding the hidey-holes of those wanted for crime. My first success was in Manchester. The house was surrounded, and I covered the back garden. When our man could not be found the house was entered and searched using a police dog. I waited outside as officers drifted out saying that he was not there, then went in to have a look myself. Some hiding places are very ingenious and the first thing that I did was to ensure that a wall has two sides. What I mean by that is that both sides of a wall should be two brick widths apart; anything more and there must be a reason. On this occasion I noticed that in the bedroom there was a fitted wardrobe and the wall behind it seemed to be very wide. I pulled all the clothes out and put them on the bed. I touched the back of the wardrobe and the thin panel covering it slid back on runners behind the dressing table. An arm came out followed by a body.

'OK mate, I'll come out.' In most cases like this the house has been searched many times and its crafty purpose-built hidey-hole not discovered.

The next one was in Liverpool where a house was searched by Liverpool detectives with our back-up. As usual the wife or girlfriend was complaining strongly about the search and swearing that she had not seen this bloke for years. As was also usual on these well-organised trips, no one had brought a torch! I went into the attic and the CID Aid or trainee followed me but without a torch there was nothing to see. I asked if someone could go back to Speke police station about half amile away and get one. This was met with much moaning from the other officers who just wanted to get away and have breakfast; they were also fed up with the woman, who was now threatening to sue them. The longer we waited the dirtier the looks I got but eventually the torch arrived. I went up into the loft and kicked the insulation about. I saw a crack in the plasterboard floor and put my nails under it. It lifted and turned out to be a homemade trap door. Shining my torch down into the narrow hole I saw our man squatting at the bottom in his underpants – the very man that the woman downstairs had not seen for years! I helped him out and shouted for someone to help him out of the loft. What they had done was to brick up the alcove that a lot of houses have in a bedroom over the stairwell, then plaster and wallpaper it to match the rest of the room. When the police arrived, he would swing into the loft, drop down the hole and pull the trap door across. This man was wanted for armed robbery; he had discharged a shotgun into the roof of a bank and the house had been searched many times without success. I accepted the congratulations humbly!

There was one other person I winkled out – as we knocked on the door, I saw a man's face behind the curtains but when we eventually got the woman to open the door he was nowhere to be seen. A small man, he had a custom-built drawer hidden under the mattress in the baby's cot. That is where we found him. I used to love the challenge; it was like playing hide and seek as a child!

Chapter Twenty-Seven

Warrington CID & a Spate of Murders

ON 2 JANUARY 1993, I was involved in a traffic accident when a boy racer in his dad's 4x4 lost it at a junction and slammed into me, my ribs were badly bruised, and the doctor forbade me from returning to work. As a result, was off work for two months. I had served four years on the RCS, so my secondment was almost up, and when I returned to work on 1 March 1993 it was to Warrington CID. I took up the post of detective sergeant on the day after the first Provo bomb was detonated on the 26 February. The first of two major incidents when the IRA set off bombs. This first bomb was at Warrington Gas Works and although a lot of damage was caused, the only casualty was a Warrington PC Mark Toker who stopped the van being driven by the bombers and was shot three times for his trouble. After a high-speed car chase. The IRA bombers were arrested on the M62 in Manchester and subsequently received prison sentences. The DC Mark Toker received the Queen's Police Medal for gallantry, the youngest holder of the medal in the country.

Under me I had two detective constables and one CID Aide. Little did we know that it was not going to be long before there was a second and far more devastating bomb blast.

Between them, on 3 March a man by the name of Reginald Price shot his common law wife, Marcelle Fitton, as she was sitting in his car outside a club in Warrington. He then turned the gun on himself. She was killed outright, but he survived. When their house was searched, some videotapes were seized, and I was nominated to take them to the intelligence section at headquarters to view them.

On the surface things looked straight forward – he had shot her and then shot himself – but there were no witnesses.

He was still alive and, if he lived, he could blame it on his partner and deny any part in the shooting. Evidence-gathering was important. With the assistance of the intelligence office staff, I set about viewing the tapes. Price was an avid amateur film-maker and there was quite a lot to go through. At the same time, another monitor in the office was being used to view the footage of the roadside cameras during the high-speed chase with the IRA bombers; there was a lot going on. I had picked what I thought to be the latest tape and it started by showing a children's party. My intelligence man was becoming bored and after the party film had ended, the tape gave the appearance of being unused, just fuzzy lines, and the counter had stopped moving. My bored expert flicked it off.

'Leave it now, that's the end of the tape, do another.'

'No, I replied, I'm going to fast forward it to the end; you can go and watch the IRA if you like!' The tape ran on, showing only the snowy mist of unused footage.

'Come on,' he said again, 'this is daft.'

'I'm taking this to the end,' I insisted, as he walked off.

My patience was unexpectedly rewarded. No more than five minutes from the end of the tape, the mist gave way to a clear image and the illuminated counter started working. The film was of Reginald Price. He was sitting in front of the camera on a chair and his hand was receding after switching it on. He then went on to say that it was his intention to shoot Marcelle and then commit suicide. About two hours of blank tape had passed before this small but extremely important snippet of film had been made. He died of his wounds later that day, but the video ensured a smooth and argument-free coroner's inquest into the death.

On Saturday 20 March I was at home in Middlewich, we had a house on the canal and I was relaxing on the canal bank when one of the detective sergeants on duty, Dick Strachan, phoned me. 'You have to come straight away, there has been another bombing.'

I couldn't believe it. Warrington is just an ordinary Cheshire town, why would it suffer this attention twice in such a short time? It has been suggested that the second bombing was as a result of the success in capturing the Provisional IRA members who caused the first incident. On this occasion, quite a few people were injured and two young boys, Johnathan Ball, aged three, and twelve-year-old Tim Parry, were killed. Two bombs were placed in litterbins in the centre of the pedestrianised town centre and set to detonate when the street would be thronged with shoppers. As no one was arrested for this outrage, the inquiry was to commence, and it would be a long and arduous one.

It was decided to split the CID office with a lot of the staff being attached to the bombing inquiry, which was given the operation name Operation Bridge; a smaller number would be left to cover the day to day running of the divisional crime investigations. I was nominated to remain on the Division and the shifts were amalgamated. Warrington had two satellite CID offices at Stockton Heath and Risley. The officers manning them were seconded to the main office and included in the shifts based there. All the CID space was taken over by the bombing operation so two Portakabins were set up in the rear car park to house the divisional CID staff. My block or shift had more detective constables with the introduction of the outstation staff, but the workload was increased accordingly.

I would frequently check the messages that were received at the police station. Missing from home enquiries, in most cases, had little to do with the CID. It was best to know about them though in case they turned out to be a bit more ominous than the usual missing teenagers.

On 29 March 1993, I saw that a 26-year-old woman had been reported missing by her parents back on the thirteenth.

'What's in this one?' I asked the station sergeant. 'She's been missing for some time!'

'Yeah, there might be something in that, her parents are worried and keep coming down to see what we're doing. I don't think there's anything to worry about though, see them if you like, they're coming in again later.'

In the afternoon, I saw Eddy Folkes and his wife, Sandra at the police station. They were very worried about their daughter Sharon. Although she was from an excellent home, Sharon Louise Cooper had led a rather seedy life once she had left. She had married a man called William John Cooper, known as John Cooper in 1991, and back in 1984 they had had a son, Christopher, who was now eight years old. When I investigated the background, I knew that this required further work. Sharon and John had lived in Longshaw Street in Warrington and John had left the family home fairly recently and moved into the Pied Bull Hotel in Newton-le-Willows, not far away. A short time later, he had removed Christopher from his school, found him another one and had the boy living with him at the Pied Bull.

The Folkes were not happy, although they perhaps saw their daughter in the same light as when she had lived with them, and not as she had later become. They did have cause for concern.

'He's been phoning us and telling us not to attempt to take Christopher back,' said Eddy, near to tears. 'Something's going on; Sharon wouldn't walk out on the lad.'

Eddy was a hard-working joiner with a broad Warrington accent. He and Sandra had had another child late in life and he was about the same age as their grandson, they also had an adult daughter.

'I will do all I can,' I assured them. 'Leave it with me; I'll be in touch as soon as anything comes to light.' They seemed happier now that someone was doing something. To be fair though, a woman of 26 going missing is not an unusual occurrence and she could not be described as vulnerable.

I briefed the lads on my block. I had two DCs, Paul Rumney and Liam Smyth, and they were a good mix. Paul was one of the new breed of detectives, he would ensure that everything was down on paper to justify his every move. When it was, he would act, but strictly by the book, no shortcuts and nothing exciting, the sort of detective better suited to major incidents, fraud, and office work. Liam was more like me, quite happy to sail by the seat of his pants and get the job done, ensuring that at the end of the day the paperwork was correct. There was room for both types in a working office and I was happy. The following day, I collected the key to Sharon's home, a terraced council-owned house that we entered via the back. The rear garden was an absolute mess with rubbish piled high everywhere. Inside was worse and as soon as we entered the living room, Liam – who did not have a particularly weak stomach – retched at the smell and the filth. We had a cursory search, as I had already decided that I wanted the job doing properly by the force dedicated search team. Whilst we were at the house, John Cooper turned up. He agreed to come to the police station with us and we asked him about his wife's disappearance. Cooper was tall and skinny with a very strange manner.

He gave us the background to their turbulent relationship. This had culminated in February when Sharon showed him an injunction, she had taken out to stop him approaching her or Christopher. It was then that he had moved out of the family home and into the Pied Bull Hotel. The obvious question was put to him.

'When did you last see Sharon?'

'It was at the beginning of March in the High Street in Newton-le-Willows,' he replied. 'She was in a blue Datsun Cherry car, alone. She saw me and pulled over.'

'What happened then?' I asked.

'She asked me if I could look after Christopher. When I asked her for how long, she wouldn't say, oh and she asked me if I would buy her car.'

'And did you?' asked Liam.

'Yes, she gave me the log book and MOT certificate.'

'What about Christopher?' I asked.

'She told me to collect him from school; she even said that if I didn't, he would be put in care.'

'So, when did you last see her?' I asked again.

'Then,' he replied. 'She got out of the car and walked off; I have never seen her since.'

What a load of rubbish, I thought. Why when she had taken out an injunction against him would she want him to take the boy and not her parents? They were able and willing to look after Christopher. It did not add up, he was lying and what we needed was something we did not have: evidence. On the day I first met the Folkes they had, with the consent of the court, removed Christopher from the school that John had arranged for him to attend. At my request, officers with special training in interviewing children were tasked with questioning Christopher about his time with John and the last time he saw his mother.

On 1 April, we visited the Pied Bull Hotel and the landlord opened John's room for us when John was out. We had the landlord's permission, and we had a good look around; it was a rather scruffy single room and there was nothing of interest there. We waited for John to return and questioned him again in the room. This time he said that he asked Sharon to sell him her car and, combined with this, there were other discrepancies in his story. I decided to take the bull by the horns.

'I'm not happy with your explanation John, some of the things you have told me are different from your statement. I will ask you direct, have you had anything to do with her disappearance?'

He replied, 'No.'

I arrested him on suspicion of abduction and took him to Warrington.

I knew he had done something, but I needed evidence. If there was any, I would find it. With Paul Rumney, I interviewed him and recorded it on tape. Some of the questions were as follows and taken from the record – I said to him:

'When was the last you saw of your wife?'

'Last I saw of her; she was walking down towards Newton train station.'

'So, she meets you in the middle of Newton-le-Willows by sheer coincidence, she stops, you have a discussion through the window, which results in you taking out of your back pocket £160.' He butted in to say that he didn't have it all with him and that he had to go to the post office to get the rest. 'So, you must have seen her later,' I suggested.

'No, she waited for me to get it.' He then went on to say that she got out of the car and handed him the keys over the roof before she set off towards the train station. He asked her if she wanted a lift, and she declined the offer. The interview continued and I pointed out that he was keeping something from us and there was something missing.

I said to him, 'Your wife has disappeared, there's no record of her anywhere. You are driving about in her car, with her coat in the back. You've taken Christopher from school off your own back at the same time as she goes missing and it is highly suspicious. It suggests that you have had something to do with her disappearance. Have you had anything to do with her disappearance?'

'No, except to give her £160,' he replied. When Paul pointed out that he did not look concerned for his wife, his reply was that he was trying not to let it show. Paul then, to illustrate my description of his work practices earlier, questioned him about driving her car without documents and did he realise that he was a menace on the road! I sat with my mouth open, motoring offences? Menace on the road? This bastard had killed his wife and I knew it!

On 2 April, I returned to the Pied Bull Hotel alone and again questioned Cooper. It was obvious to me that he was hiding something, and I wanted to find out what it was, but he would say nothing. He did say he was planning on leaving for Scotland in the very near future.

Chapter Twenty-Eight

A Long Interview with a Bizarre Murderer

That afternoon, I stood in the restroom at Warrington police station playing the fruit machine, the television was on at the other side of the room and the news was showing. I was not really listening to it, at least until I saw a film of the sand dunes at Ainsdale, near Southport. A woman's body had been found partly decomposed by a man walking his dog. I knew immediately that it was Sharon. Despite having a winning line on the fruit machine, I ran upstairs and phoned the incident room at Southport police station. I asked them for a description of the body, and it tied in with that of Sharon. Now it was time for CID politics.

'Where was she murdered, on Cheshire or on Liverpool?' We currently had a major investigation into two bombings and Detective Superintendent 'Skippy' Anderton, the Senior Investigating Officer, was expressing concern at our ability to deal with it. If Sharon had been murdered in Warrington and then taken to Ainsdale, it would be a Cheshire job. I told him that the Liverpool body was almost certainly connected with Warrington, and I wanted to arrest John Cooper.

'Don't do any such thing,' he ordered. 'We haven't got the manpower to deal with that.'

He contacted Detective Superintendent Albert Kirby in Liverpool, the current Senior Investigator of the dunes body investigation and it was agreed that Liverpool would deal with it and arrest John as soon as the body had been formally identified. I pointed out that he was going to leave for Scotland, especially now as he would know the body had been found.

'That can't be helped,' said 'Skippy,' 'let Liverpool deal.' I could appreciate his problem, with the bombing investigation ongoing there just was not the manpower to set up an incident room and allocate a load of detectives to it, even if technically it was a Cheshire job. I arranged to take Eddie Folkes and his other daughter to Southport, and I got Paul and Liam together.

'I want you both to go and sit on the Pied Bull, don't let John go anywhere. Don't lock him up unless you think he's leaving the area. Stay there until Liverpool come and arrest him, I don't care if he knows you are there so long as he doesn't get away.'

This was against the instructions I had been given, but there was no way I was going to let him escape now. As I set off to Southport, they did stick with him; Liam even followed him to the chip shop! When Liverpool detectives arrived, it was left to them.

While this was going on, poor Eddy was helping us to identify Sharon. He was devastated. Although he had suspected it all along, confirmation was not easy to bear. The body was so decomposed that the main form of identification was a rather unique wristwatch that she had been wearing. Eddie and his daughter were taken home and I stayed with Albert Kirby. Albert was a household name at the time as he was also the Senior Investigating Officer on the infamous murder of the toddler James Bulger in Bootle a month or so earlier.

'Cooper has been arrested, come on,' said Albert. 'I want this bastard to see you when he's brought in.' We went down to the cells, and Detective Inspector Peter Halpin brought him in. Cooper looked no different, I have never seen a person with such a continuously bland look about him, he was expressionless. Arrangements had been made between the Cheshire and Liverpool superintendents for me to remain on the investigation and jointly interview Cooper with Peter Halpin. This was quite an honour. I remain very good friends with Peter, who is now a driving test examiner with the Ministry of Transport.

COOPER'S TIME WAS UP and at 12.52pm the next day we started questioning him. He had a local solicitor who, during the first part of the interview, had to be warned about interfering and going beyond what he was entitled to do. As the day progressed, Cooper continued to deny any knowledge – answering questions in a strange monotone manner – while the solicitor became less obstructive. He put pertinent questions to Cooper in an attempt to get at the truth, but his client continued to deny any knowledge.

It was not until late in the evening that Cooper finally admitted strangling Sharon in her car in Hermitage Green Lane, between Warrington and Newton-le-Willows. When he finally cracked it was in that same voice. The atmosphere in the room was electric, with a feral smell emanating from this strange pale, gangling murderer, and it was hard to keep talking coherently afterwards. The room was wired up to a speaker outside where the other officers on the inquiry, including I think Albert, were listening. They had to control their euphoria at the admission and settle for high fives and facial expressions. The interviewing finished for the night and Albert had arranged for me to stay in a hotel near the police station. There was a debrief and we all went to the hotel for a drink: that had been one hard interview. Peter and I were mentally shattered, but on a high and it would take a drink to bring us down to earth again. Albert bought the first round, and we had a very good drink. As the night wore on the local detectives left, leaving Peter and me. The last thing I remember was playing darts with the locals and constantly missing the board.

The following day, we continued the interviews and although Cooper admitted murdering Sharon, he kept many secrets. He had still shown no remorse and his personality or demeanour had not changed. Neither humour nor depression had shown itself on his face. He said that he had met Sharon on the High Street as he had told us, on the morning of 5 March, but then she had driven him to Hermitage Green Lane where he had strangled her. He said that it was to stop her from strangling him! He had then driven around for several days with her body in the boot before he took her to the dunes where he buried her.

On the pretence of taking Christopher to play in the dunes in the days and weeks that followed, he had left the boy and gone to check that the body was still buried. When Sharon's body was found, she was wearing only one shoe.

At 3.45pm on 4 April, we took Cooper to Hermitage Green Lane in order for him to point out where he had killed her. On the way, he was handcuffed to me in the back of the car, still that strange humourless character. When I made some small joke, he suddenly started to laugh in a horrible cackling way. It was out of all contexts to the humour in the joke and went on for quite a while. I found it very weird and spooky, and I know that Peter did too. He stopped this laughing as quickly as he started and reverted to his macabre demeanour.

At Hermitage Green Lane, Cooper directed us to a disused driveway and indicated the location. Officers from the Merseyside Operational Support Division had also joined us; they were going to search the area fully.

One of them called to us from an area about 50 feet from the indicated scene of the murder. He had found a woman's shoe. It was pointed out to Cooper, who identified it as Sharon's but could not explain how it had got so far from the alleged 'scene'. It matched the shoe found with the body.

Eddy and Sandra Folkes were relieved that Cooper had been charged but when he later appeared in Liverpool Crown Court, they were less than happy. Cooper was charged with murder but found guilty of manslaughter and sentenced to seven years in prison. This upset the Folkes greatly, especially Sandra who it must be said became obsessed that a miscarriage of justice had occurred. Her health suffered and for several years they campaigned for further action against him. I knew that he had by no means told us fully what had happened on that fateful day but there was no further evidence to support any more police action. The prosecuting barrister was Mr Richard Henriques, QC who, the following week, was to officiate in the trial of the two young murderers of James Bulger. DC Rumney went on to make Detective Superintendent in the Greater Manchester Force and Liam spent some time on the National Crime Squad before emigrating to Australia.

Chapter Twenty-Nine

Suicide and arresting a police officer

LIFE AND THE BOMBING ENQUIRES WENT ON. I continued to work as part of the team covering day-to-day crime. It was quite cosy in the two Portakabins and did not interfere with our work.

One of the jobs during this period was a double suicide – a man called Brian Holt had driven his car into a Warrington field with his wife Karen in the passenger seat. A rubber hose was passed from the exhaust pipe to the slightly opened back window and they just sat there with the engine running, listening to the radio. Death by carbon monoxide poisoning is not a very pleasant way to die either on purpose, as in this case, or in the many accidental deaths that occur each year. After a while in the car, they would have become drowsy but very soon they would pass the point of no return: still capable of thought but incapable of any movement, so if at the last minute they changed their mind they would find their bodies unable to move and slowly die. This case was made even sadder because the word was out that the man was a police informant: he had been threatened numerous times, supposedly leading him with his wife to commit suicide. This had to be investigated as the police would have some explaining to do if it bore any substance.

The rules relating to officers using informants is now quite well controlled and everything must leave a confidential paper trail. The informant is given a nom de plume and any payments require total control and the involvement of the handler's supervisor. If this man *was* a registered informant there would be written evidence of the fact somewhere – and there wasn't. The rumour mill had spread around the estate and the man, although innocent of the allegations, took his own life and that of his wife. It was all very sad really, but I was able to inform the inquest that he was not an informant and maybe, just maybe, some of the bullies would have some pangs of guilt.

At least this method of suicide is relatively tidy as far as the officers handling it are concerned, unlike the detective inspector mentioned earlier who dowsed himself in petrol, or the frequent incidents of people throwing themselves in front of trains. I had not been in the police long when I was called to my first suicide of this type, or maybe it was an accident – either way a man was struck by an express train heading for Crewe and his head burst on the windscreen of the engine. The driver was, naturally, traumatised. We then had to walk along the track picking up the bits and putting them in a bag, not very pleasant for the police, the driver or the man's family who could not see his body one final time.

On that occasion the force photographer took photos although at night it was hard to see what the bits were. When he developed the photos, he found that he had caught a mouse nibbling a severed hand. He used that gruesome photo in many lectures to new policemen.

Warrington police station had within its boundaries The No1 District Police Training Centre at Bruche where I had attended and been trained. Because of its location, we dealt with any crime committed by the students there. On 22 June 1993, Dave Wilcock, the DI, and I went at the request of the commandant.

'We have had an alleged offence of indecent assault committed by a Manchester officer,' said one of the staff members, 'the Manchester Complaints and Discipline Department are on the way.' Within a very short time, a superintendent and inspector joined us from that department.

'We just want to get rid,' said the superintendent, 'we don't want twats like this in the force.'

'Well, we'll deal with it,' said Dave, indicating that it was our responsibility until we said otherwise. The recruit had been put into an unoccupied house on the campus until we arrived. We had arranged for statements to be taken from the policewoman and her friends by officers from Warrington.

On entering the room, the young officer jumped to attention. He was in full immaculate uniform with the red lanyard of a class leader, and he was also the class drill instructor. He appeared the perfect trainee, both in manner and dress.

'We have come from Warrington CID,' I said and introduced Dave and myself.

'Sir,' he replied in smart military fashion.

Dave said to him, 'We are here because an allegation of indecent assault has been made against you.'

'I thought this was because I'd been in the girls' block,' he replied, looking questioningly from me to Dave and back again.

'What happened?' asked Dave.

'I was in her room, I'll admit that, but I thought she was happy about what happened.' He retained his strong military bearing and looked through us at the wall.

'There's no way that we are arresting you and taking you back looking like that,' I said. 'But arrest you is what we have got to do.'

Dave told him that he was under arrest and cautioned him, then we took him to his room to get changed out of his uniform. Prior to joining the police, he had been in a glamorous job and had enjoyed the adulation of women. Whilst at Bruche, he had apparently attempted to get a policewoman to masturbate him. She had declined and a few days later he had gone to her room whilst she was in bed and asked her once again.

She again declined and told him to sod off, to which he replied. 'Well, I'll do it myself then' At this, he knelt astride her on her bed and masturbated himself.

When he left, she went to the shower room in her nightie and was found by some of the other policewomen showering with the garment still on. They questioned her and she told them what had happened and that she didn't want to complain as it would destroy his career. They disagreed and without her consent reported the matter the following day, setting the ponderous wheels of justice in motion.

'This man is a trainee police officer at Bruche, and we have arrested him for indecent assault.' I related the facts to the custody sergeant as I had to do, and he was booked in.

'I don't want him in the cells,' I said to Dave, and he told me that the superintendent's office was empty, so I took him in there. We sat down and the officer asked me what would happen. I told him that he would be interviewed and that if he admitted it fully, he could get a caution. I added that if he did not admit it, he would be going to the Crown Court and, in view of the evidence, he would have little chance of winning.

'So, if I tell the truth and admit what I did, I will get a caution and then I can go back to Bruche?' he said, looking at me hopefully.

'No,' I said. 'Your police career ended last night when you went into that room and did what you did.' I told him this truthfully, but it was not what he wanted to hear. At this he broke down in tears.

'What can I tell my wife?' he sobbed.

'We won't be telling her anything,' I replied helpfully. 'Just say that you could not hack it, or you did not enjoy it and you have given up.' He looked at me with tears rolling down his cheeks.

'I absolutely love this job, I am top of the course and every weekend I have been telling her what a brilliant career it is, God, what am I going to do?'

There was nothing to say, there was nothing supportive that I could tell him; he had been an absolute idiot and what he had done could never be excused.

Dave and I interviewed him on tape, and he admitted it. On completion, he was formally cautioned by the duty inspector. The representatives of the Greater Manchester Police Complaints and Discipline Department, who had been patiently waiting, put him in their car. They took him back to Bruche were they collected his belongings, drove him to his home town and then dumped him around the corner from his house. An embarrassment to the police force had been dealt with. That one stupid act had destroyed the career of a promising recruit. He was not the first and he would not be the last.

Still in 1993 I woke up in Middlewich where we lived and looked out of the window. Where's my bike gone I shouted? When I went to bed it was in the drive, now it's gone.'

The 650cc motorbike that I commuted to work on had been taken from the front garden and I hadn't heard a thing.

I got on to the insurance company and sent them a photograph. Good news, they would pay me £100 more than I paid for it: now for the fun, let's buy another!

I had been to a few car auctions, but never a bike auction and there was one advertised in one of my bike magazines. Rose and I set off for a look. The bikes were in lines in the auction hall in Holmfirth and one really caught my eye, it looked beautiful. It was smaller than I wanted really, but it was pristine. A Kawasaki 454 LTD in black and silver with red piping, it was about six years old and a very tidy bike indeed.

'Can I see it running?' I asked the man.

'No, I'm afraid we're not allowed to start them in here, we've had it running though, sweet as a nut!'

'Good enough for me,' I thought (well, I always was naïve!).

I got it for £900, not bad, as it looked an excellent bike for that money. Now to try it. No luck.

'Mr, this bike won't start,' I said.

'Not to worry, probably flooded, we can deliver it for you if you want,' and this they did.

When I tried it at home, it just would not go so I had it collected by a bike shop for checking over, servicing, testing, and replacing the rubber bung thing on the end of the mirror!

A week later I phoned them. 'How's the bike going?'

'No problem, we have serviced it and replaced the rubber bung thing; you can have it back tomorrow.' Brilliant, the following day I phoned back.

'Can I come for my bike now?'

'Err, I don't know how to say this.'

'Go on!'

'Well, we tried to start it and it wouldn't, so we took the plugs out and turned the engine, and all the oil came out of one of the plug holes. So, we took the head off…'

'And?'

'Well, one of the piston chambers had a piston in it.'

'And the other?'

'A biro!'

'A biro, you mean a biro pen, a biro with ink in it?'

'Err, yes, a biro pen. This engine has been blown up, it's dead, it won't fix, and basically it's fu….'

'Yes, I get the message; can you get a replacement engine?'

It was agreed that they would get a replacement and they did. The bike was then as good as new, and it had cost me a total of £1,700. Still not outrageous, but I had been mugged and wasn't having it. Someone had re-sealed the engine leaving a pen in the empty pot to take the piss and polished the bike up. I started my detective work!

Luckily a bike trader had put the bike into the auction. That is different from an ordinary punter; bike traders can't do that and get away with it. I contacted him. It transpired that he had suffered the same fate as me – he had bought it for £500 down south, sussed that the bike was a lemon and brought it up north, putting it in an auction here where I had bought it.

'Do the same thing,' he suggested helpfully. 'Put it in another auction!'

Well, I decided that the buck would have to stop or eventually the bike would become a collector's piece bouncing from auction to auction. I would seek legal advice.

As result proceedings were launched in the Small Claims Court, but my detective work continued. I traced the lad who had put the bike in the auction down south. I told him that legal action was being taken against the dealer who had bought it.

'If he loses,' I told him, 'he will probably be coming after you. If I lose, I probably will.' He was not happy but told me of the bike's history.

It had been imported by an American Air Force Serviceman and used by his wife until she blew it up on the motorway. He had it taken to a garage and, when it was discovered that it needed a new engine, he sold them the bike for £100, left it there and went back to his air base for some hamburgers and grits! A soft lad working for the garage then decided to make a few bob and he polished up the bike, re-sealed the engine and made it look nice. He put it in the auction and the dealer bought it. The rest we know.

The years passed as they always do when the slow wheels of justice are turned, and the dealer denied liability. He sold a bike that wasn't of saleable quality and as a dealer he was not exempt from this requirement just because it was an auction. I got plenty of help from the auction management, although they could not remember telling me that they had started it up and saying, 'it runs sweet as a nut!' In the meantime, I had the bike and it was a good one – there were no light switches, because it was a US import, and the indicators were illuminated orange lights until activated, then they flashed. The previous owner had lowered the back end and it would not, without the use of a crane, go on to the main stand. I was trying to pull this relatively small bike on to the main stand one day and I was struggling in the yard of the police station. Two big police motorcyclists came over and intimated that I was a big tart because I couldn't lift it. Being macho, they tried, and it took both of them to do it. They went away red faced to polish their jackboots and I took the main stand off and threw it away!

Because I was doing the suing, the dealer could say where he wanted the hearing. He plumped for Worksop some 100 miles away, so I had to go on the train. A civil hearing like this is very informal – you sit around a conference table and the judge, in our case a woman, deliberates. The dealer started out by demanding that there was no case to answer, as it was an auction. If the judge overruled this and decided there was a case to answer, it would have to go to a higher court because it may result in a 'stated case' (meaning that the decision would affect the running of auctions and dealers really would have to stop ripping people off!). We went outside whilst she considered the matter and I spoke with the dealer. I pointed out that he didn't have a chance of winning, and why was he fighting for the sake of a few hundred pounds? He asked me how much I was talking about, and I told him. He agreed to pay me that amount; I think it was about £800. We went back into the room and the judge said that she could deal with the case, at which the dealer told her that we had discussed the matter outside, and he was prepared to pay. She said that she would formalise it and we could all go home. I got my money back and I had a good bike into the bargain. I don't know if the dealer went looking for the soft lad who had started it all off in the first place – I know that I would have if I had lost! There is only one moral to this story: when buying at auction, beware; there are loads of 'soft lads' out there who are quite prepared to rip people off and it is the easiest place to do it. One of my first magazines was this story in the Used Bike Guide. A glossy magazine. By then I had sold the bike and the only photo that I had with it was a photo of Rose sitting on it. We went to London and in the newsagents at Euston the magazine was on sale. That was the first time that Rose saw herself as the centrefold in the Used Bike Guide. Any sailor reading this will know why she was not too happy, albeit quite proud.

Life continued at Warrington, as did the bombing inquiry. A temporary compound had been built in the large drill hall and the bombing inquiry was controlled from there while we carried on using the Portakabins. It's amazing how small bits of information, notes and sundry reports can suddenly develop into something serious. My next explosive message was from the DI, Dave Wilcock. It simply asked me to interview a well-known gangster from Widnes who was alleging abuse at a care home when he was a boy. Ho-hum, more mundane work I thought. I was very wrong.

I didn't know it at the time but, as you got a flavour of it in Chapter One, I was about to start the second biggest paedophile inquiry into child abuse in care homes in Great Britain: Operation Granite. I was about to do what had not been done by many police officers and agencies in the past. I was to take the complaint seriously – and act upon it.

Chapter Thirty

Back to Divisional CID a nasty assault and an old paedo

I REMAINED ON OPERATION GRANITE for about eighteen months and by then I had had enough. I wasn't happy with the way the operation was going or its management. Frank Ball had taken over as the DCI, but he left the running of the operation to the DI Terry Oates. It was all so delicate and yet the instructions given to avoid false disclosures did not seem to have the same priority. It was not running as I would have liked, and I was finding it more and more difficult to work with the DI. Combined with that, spending every day talking to men who had been abused when they were younger, and to the extent that I knew went on, was heartrending.

One of my first jobs when I returned to divisional CID duties was to attend an assault in Penketh. As a police officer, you see all sorts of things the public never have the opportunity to see but it does not stop you from being amazed. Some people die after being punched lightly; others are assaulted to such a terrible extent that they should never recover, but they do. This was one of the latter. A woman who had separated from her husband had gone back to the family home to catch the pet cats and take them to her new house. She had gone with her friend, and they were looking for the cats at the side of the house.

Suddenly the other woman felt a sharp pain in her shoulder and turned to see her friend's estranged husband striking her with a ball-pein hammer with an extra long shaft. As she shouted a warning, he attacked his ex-wife, hammering her around the head and smashing her skull like he would an egg. She went to the floor, and he continued, even snapping the hammer shaft in the process. People gathered round, but he had completely lost it and they were frightened of going near him, despite the fact that he was obviously trying to murder her.

Eventually he stopped and she was left lying on the floor. He was covered from head to foot in her blood; he looked as if someone had thrown a full bucket of blood at him. I arrested him. The ambulance attended and the wife and her friend were taken to Warrington General Hospital. I visited her there the following day and, miraculously, she was able to sit up and talk. I had seen photographs back in the office of her head after it had been shaved and there were over 30 hammer strike marks, most of which had broken the skull. She was then able to tell me what it had been like.

She had been conscious throughout and after she went down, she kept her eyes shut as she knew that if she opened them, she would see bits of her skull on the footpath, and it would frighten her. She could remember the hammer breaking as it hit her head. After this happened, she felt him get hold of her head by putting his fingers through the shattered bone in the space between the bone and her brain and pulling on the remaining skull as you would pull open a drawer. When I took her statement, I must admit that I deliberately left this bit out as it sounded too far-fetched. It was true though and at court the barrister told me that I should have included it. She remained in hospital for a while, but amazingly she went on to make a full recovery.

When I interviewed her husband a college lecturer, he said that he could not remember doing it. I charged him with attempted murder, and he pleaded guilty and received eight years in prison from Judge Robin David at Chester Crown Court – the most respected and senior judge on the Cheshire and North Wales Circuit. I had been before him many times and he was very fair. On this occasion he had me doing something that I have never done before that I found quite funny. Normally, now that we have taped interviews, when giving evidence the interviewing officer will read out a transcript of the taped interview. This is usually done with the officer being the interviewer and the barrister being the prisoner. Judge David changed the rules for me; he wanted me to read it all out! This meant that I had to changes voices.

'What is your name?' (My own voice)

'Billy Smith,' (me putting on a different voice).

This was done in open court and luckily the offence was so serious that no one giggled.

Having returned to the humdrum day to day work of a detective sergeant, I thought that my days dealing with sad paedophiles were over, but having gained all that knowledge on Operation Granite, I was to be called upon to deal with a lot of the serious paedophile offences within the division.

The next job didn't take long in arriving. There was concern for a young teenager who had been living rough in Blackpool. He was known to earn cash as a rent boy on occasions and one of the enquiries was to see an old man called David Ernest Waterhouse in Warrington who was suspected of having dealings with him. I went with DC Alex Kane to the pensioner's bungalow. We knocked at the door and there was no answer. We knocked again more forcibly with still no answer. After that I lifted the letterbox flap and politely pointed out that if the door was not opened, I would put the bastard in! It worked and we were faced with an old man of seventy-seven, a man who had been a bomber pilot in the war and had served with distinction, a man who was well-known paedophile. In the hall, there was a haversack full of clothing. When asked whose it was, he confirmed that it belonged to the missing boy who had stayed there for a while but had now left.

'Do you mind if we have a look around?' I asked politely.

'Err, no,' he replied, knowing full well that I was going to anyway. Alex went to the bathroom in the small bungalow, and I searched the bedroom. The large tub of Vaseline on the bedside table raised my suspicions and were raised further by a shout from Alex. I went to the bathroom and found a half-naked young teenage boy hiding behind the door. It was obviously the missing rent boy, we thought, but it was another boy, a friend of the missing one – a boy that the heroic bomber pilot and RAF officer had just finished having his evil way with. He was arrested and admitted his guilt. Despite being 77 years old and not in good health, he was sentenced to seven years in prison.

Right let's have a rest from nastiness now and talk of something with a bit of humour (we can go back to the nasty side later with possibly my worst paedophile investigation).

I had been on the new course for handcuffs and baton at RAF Sealand at Chester and my partner for the day had been the sergeant in charge of the Stockton Heath Initiative Team, Sgt Grant Ardern. Shortly after, he came up to see me.

'You've got a bit of bottle Paul; how do you fancy going under cover in a brothel?'

Me, I thought, me a front-line detective sergeant doing work like that. 'Yes alright, where is it?' I replied. I must admit that I am a big believer in legalising prostitution and brothels; I think that if they were legal, it would cut down on the number of sexual offences committed against women. However, in this case there had been many complaints from the neighbours, and something had to be done about it. The fruit and veg shop downstairs was not happy about the noise and customers were on one hand complaining, and some offering to take the willy-shaped vegetables upstairs as they may like to make use of them!

'Don't be like John,' warned Grant, 'remember he did a similar job and shagged the prossie, it cocked up all the evidence!' I remembered the case and John, whose surname I will keep to myself, still gets the piss taken.

'Hello, is that the massage parlour?'

'Yes, can we help?'

'I am just passing through and I saw your ad, can I come up now?'

'Yes, no problem, do you know where we are?'

I went up the steel fire escape at the back of the shops leading to the massage parlour and met the girl sitting at a reception desk. After paying my £10 I was shown into a small room with a bed and told to undress to my shorts. A few minutes later an attractive girl joined me in a white doctor's coat that failed to cover all of her knickers.

'What would you like?' she asked as she started to massage my back in a lackadaisical sort of way.

'What do you charge?' I replied, trying to sound like the sort of businessman who uses massage parlours and whose wife does not understand him.

She gave me a verbal list of the services that were provided which ranged across the full spectrum of sexual activity. By now the excuse for a massage was over and I told her that I did not have much time, I wanted to have a look at the place first but I would be back. I assured her that I would ask for her and I left. I completed a witness statement and gave it to the sergeant.

It took a while for them to raid the place and before doing so they decided that they would send in a second undercover man to make sure they were still at it. This lad was not quite as covert. He walked up the steps to the woman at the desk and asked what services they provided. When she started to tell him, he took out his pocket book and wrote them down – not surprisingly the girl said later that she knew he was a policeman. As a result of this, I told the sergeant that he should use the initials of his squad, the **S**tockton **H**eath **I**nitiative **T**eam as a letterhead. It was a successful raid though. Whilst they were searching the place a man came clip-clopping up the fire escape. He was met by a policeman in uniform.

'Yes, can I help you?' asked the officer.

'Err, no, it's alright, I just wondered where these steps went.'

'Oh,' said the officer, you weren't coming to the brothel then?'

'Good Lord no,' replied the man self-righteously, 'as if I would!'

'That's alright then,' said the officer, smiling and bending the truth slightly. 'We've been videoing the door for six months.' The man turned and clip-clopped down the metal fire escape.

Then clip clop clip, he came back up again.

'Err, I may have come once or twice,' he said sheepishly.

'Bugger off,' said the officer and the man went off back down the fire escape after an assurance that his wife would not be visited.

Shortly after, another client came up and was met by a female officer in plain clothes at the desk.

'I've come for the usual,' he said excitedly.

'I am afraid we have different girls here today,' replied the officer. 'It is a sort of theme day; do you like big women?'

'Oh yes,' replied the man rubbing his hands, saliva sliding down his chin.

'What about uniforms?' asked the officer.

'Yes, that as well,' replied the man, hardly able to contain himself. He was directed to a room where a policewoman with a leaning to corpulence and in full uniform was reclining on a bed in a sort of Cleopatra pose. That was probably the last brothel the poor man would ever visit.

The woman who owned it was charged with permitting prostitution and everyone was happy, everyone except the customers who all had wives that didn't understand them.

For the second time my wife Rose told me off for getting involved in things which were a bit rude. She had told me off in the past for the whipping incident and she would tell me off on one more occasion when I went to a stag night and ended up on the stage at Foo Foo's in Manchester with my trousers down!

Dave Wilcox was still the detective inspector at Warrington and with him I would interview the prospective trainee detectives, known as CID Aides. If successful, they would join the CID as trainees for six months and would be placed with an experienced detective constable. As I was involved in the interviewing, I tended to pick the best of the bunch for my block.

Mine was a good block and included Debbie Bunker, the epitome of a ladette and a new breed of woman who was one of the lads. She would tell the most risqué stories about her lifestyle and enjoy burping contests and other such male oriented activities. We all got on well together and regularly went drinking in Warrington as a team.

Chapter Thirty-One

On the Tail of a Nasty Paedophile

DURING THIS TIME ONE of my last and probably most nasty paedophile inquiry came along. A prisoner in Risley Prison requested to see someone and I was asked to go. Risley prison was once a remand centre but by then was a full prison. I took DC Phil Hyde with me, and we met a prisoner there. The reason that he was there was sad. He was a soldier and due to marital difficulties, he had gone AWOL. One day he was alone at home with his baby when he heard a car stopping outside and thought they were coming for him, so he grabbed his nine-month-old son and ran upstairs to hide. In his panic, he bumped the child on the stairs on the way up and caused a slight injury. It was his intention to plead guilty assault and going AWOL and it was his first offence. He had been bailed but had then contacted his wife, which was in breach of the bail conditions, so had been sent to prison. I asked him what he wanted to tell me, and he said that when he was a child his father abused him.

There followed a horrendous story. When he was five or six his father forced him to have oral sex, and this went on to further abuse. I could not possibly put into writing details of this abuse as it is too horrible and far exceeds anything that I had heard from my time on Operation Granite. As a result of the abuse, he started to wet the bed. His father then made his two brothers urinate into a cup each morning and he had to drink it. He was then made to stand naked in the unheated garage for two hours every morning throughout the winter and summer. He had two older brothers and he said that they were also abused, sometimes all at the same time. After a while he was made to eat excreta and, in his own shocking words, 'I don't know how many times he did this, but after a while I would look forward to drinking the urine to get rid of the taste.' This went on for two or three years until his father split up with their mother and moved out. After that, abuse occurred intermittently when his father collected him for a visit.

I told him that if his brothers corroborated what he had said, we would have a case but without corroboration, after all this time we would be struggling. One brother was in the Army in England and the other in Northern Ireland. To be honest, the things he said had sickened us both that much that we didn't know if anyone would believe it, though I was quite sure he was telling the truth. We had heard how his father would have all three boys on the bed and he would stand there making each of them have oral sex with him. Could any normal person imagine a father doing that to his children?

We arranged to travel to the Army camp where the second oldest brother corroborated his story. We then caught the plane to Londonderry to have a pre - arranged meeting with the eldest brother. His wife picked us up at the airport and drove us to their married quarter. They were a lovely couple and she had prepared sandwiches and tea for us. Afterwards, I took a statement from him and again he corroborated what his other brothers had said. After another cup of tea, they drove us to the hotel in which we were to spend the night.

This story, as you can see, is completely horrific and to lighten the mood before we go further, I would like to tell a side story to our visit to Londonderry. After we were dropped us off at our hotel the eldest brother gave us a word of advice:

'If you're going out tonight.' he warned,' pointing up the road, 'go that way, don't go the other way, it leads to Londonderry.' The Northern Ireland troubles were still ongoing and certain places were no-go areas. A relative of a detective constable from the RUC owned the hotel and Phil had made the arrangements. We were to settle in, have a meal and he would join us for a drink. Oh, how innocent that sounds. But in those days in Northern Ireland everything was not that simple. We had our meal and went into the bar for a drink. By 11pm we had drunk loads and the bar, which was full of farmers, was very noisy. The DC had not shown up. We were just deciding to call it a night and go to bed when there was a loud noise as the door crashed open and three men came in. One was the DC, complete with earrings and long hair. The other was a tall man (we never did find out what he did) and the third man was a small Orangeman from Glasgow who was a lorry driver and was dressed in a two-piece navy-blue suit and tie.

We were greeted effusively in the way that only drunks can greet each other.

'Come on lads,' said the DC, 'We're taking you into town for some fecken' shwally and women, let's get the fec outa here.'

We started to walk through the crowd and as the little lorry driver passed a brassy blonde that he had never seen in his life before he shouted, 'Go on yer fucken' hoor,' at her. As she started to get up we all ran for it with the sound of an angry woman pushing tables over to get to us. In the car park the little lorry driver started to urinate over the parked cars, shouting as he did 'Here's a Fenian car, here's another Fenian car, fec the feckin' Fenians!' as each car was blessed with his own particular brand of holy water. The mad woman neared us shouting obscenities just as we reached a Ford Sierra Cosworth with a massive aerofoil on the back and climbed in. The lorry driver, after wagging his hose pipe at the rapidly approaching blonde and calling her a feckin hoor again, jumped into the front passenger seat. The DC started the car and we roared out of the car park on to the main road, leaving the blonde standing in a shower of gravel waving her fists. Within no time at all we were doing ninety miles an hour-plus with our heads pinned against the headrest by the g-force. At the same time the little lorry driver was telling us in detail how the DC had only just got out of hospital after crashing his last car and being on a life support machine for months. All very reassuring.

Phil then made an observation, 'Err, we were told not to go this way, it leads to Londonderry?'

'That's where the fun is,' he reassured us, though we were not reassured, not reassured at all. In fact, we were starting to have doubts about coming out with them.

'If anyone asks,' I said, 'what religion is it best to be?' We were further un-reassured with the reply.

'Just don't let them hear yer feckin' accents.'

We continued on our way at a ridiculous speed and eventually drove into the rear of some ominous looking tenements covered in graffiti. The car stopped and we got out. It was like a scene from A Clockwork Orange. We were smack in the middle of a sink estate in Londonderry, in an area controlled by the Protestant Ulster Freedom Fighters.

'Surely, you're not leaving your car here?' I ventured in amazement.

'Safer here than anywhere,' was the reply as we set off through the back alleys with the little lorry driver kicking all the gates making the dogs bark and inviting the shout of 'Fec off' from within. Eventually we reached the street and crossed it to a nightclub where the DC was ushered through by the bouncers. Many people greeted him; all who knew that he was in the police. The place was full of rough types and men in Union Jack T-shirts and high boots. As I was sheepishly sitting down a body landed at my feet with a recently smashed nose. It did not stay there long though; it got up and went running off after its assailant. We had a drink and the DC, who was not as daft as he looked, told us of his life. He lived alone in a flat and he knew that one day they would come for him, too many of his mates had died. He kept a number of guns in his flat and his service revolver under his pillow.

'Don't you carry it round with you?' I asked, remembering that I had heard that policemen's wives carried their guns when their husbands were not using them. He replied that he never did as it could be taken off him and it didn't mind who it shot at. It was apparent that despite the macho, cowboy image, he knew what was going on around him. The tall lad came over and whispered to him. As a result, he suggested we go downstairs as people were noticing us.

We went downstairs for more of the same. It was a proper nightclub with a disco. The atmosphere and feeling of danger was stifling, I decided to stand with my back to the wall and look hard. Phil was chatting to a girl in PVC trousers with a bare midriff when the little lorry driver stopped insulting just about everyone for a minute and came over.

'Tell yer mate, she's the tart of a UFF Godfather, fecken leave it!' I pulled Phil to one side, told him and he backed off instantly. The little lorry driver went back to taunting a six-foot four fireman.

At closing time, with the rest of the clientele, we moved out on to the footpath and by now the little lorry driver was dancing around the big fireman offering to fight.

'Look at that prick,' said the DC. He had seen the little lorry driver and at the same time realised that the fireman he was taunting was the one who had dragged him from the wreckage of his car when he had nearly died. He went over and apologised for his mate's behaviour and the lorry driver went over to taunt someone else.

'Right,' said the DC, 'off to my flat now for some more shwally.'

Both Phil and I felt that we'd had enough of this lifestyle and said we had to get back because we had to get up in the morning and we would have a busy day. We omitted to mention that we were wimps compared to these brave Ulster policemen. I suggested that we get a taxi.

'Yea has to be careful about that,' said our friend. 'Get the wrong one and y'ell be over there with holes in your knees or even worse.'

He pointed across the valley to the republican area.

'Even worse?' I said. 'You mean dead?'

'Dead if you're lucky,' he replied. I wondered what they could do that was worse than being dead!

'They may do a 50/50 on yew,' he continued. 'They shoot you in the small of your back; you either die or spend the rest of yer life paralysed.'

Oh, we thought, wondering again what we were doing in this place that God had abandoned.

'Come on, I'll sort ye oot,' he said, walking over to a small and aged uniformed inspector with a big gun. After a few quiet words we were taken to the front of the queue by the inspector. Two people about to get into a taxi were pulled away and told to sod off and we were ushered into it.

'All the best lads,' said our DC giving the taxi driver the fare from his own wallet and telling him where to go. An eccentric cavalier with strange friends, a wild lifestyle and a job that was far removed from us cosseted mainland policemen. Probably one of the bravest men I have ever met. The following week, when we were safely at home, I saw a news bulletin with a film of the nightclub and the chippy round the corner from it. Someone had been shot dead outside and lay in a pool of blood.

We had our evidence against the boys' father, and he was to be arrested. We knew he was a bus driver with Warrington Corporation, and I decided to lock him up at his place of work. If we didn't get an admission from him before he spoke with a solicitor, it was probable he would make no replies with PACE now in force. This would mean that the boys would have to be brought before the court. There is no doubt that he would be found guilty, but the witnesses would go through hell, and I didn't want that. It was time to invoke the Ways and Means Act again: I wanted to ensure that the boys did not have to be grilled in court and the solicitor did not recommend a course of action that would ensure a big wage packet for him at the end of the day. Not to mention the eventual sentence being harsher for his client, the father!

At 11.15am on Monday 9 December 1996 we went to the Warrington bus depot and were told by the inspector that the father was due in. As his bus pulled up, we went over to him. He was a middle aged apparently respectable man, a man who would never be taken for a paedophile. I told him that I was arresting him on suspicion of gross indecency and buggery on his three sons when they were young boys.

'I can't believe this,' he replied. 'I don't know what you mean, I haven't done anything, I honestly haven't done anything.'

We got in the car, and I suggested it would be easier on all concerned if he told the truth. In order to have more time, I said we were going to take him to his home to search it. The power is there under PACE to search the person and his premises after arrest. He agreed to this, and we went to his pleasant small flat. At my suggestion he went to make us a brew, a bizarre suggestion you may think but good practical detective work. He looked calm on the surface, but it was easy to see that he was fully aware that his comfortable lifestyle had gone forever. His past had finally caught up with him and he was in deep shit.

'What have they said?' he asked. I told him that they had all alleged offences of serious sexual assault against him. He asked if he could speak to his wife and I told him he could do that from the police station, he was still separated from her and had been for several years.

He sat down, put his head in his hands and replied, 'I'm finished aren't I, I'll lose my job and everything, what will happen to me?'

I told him that I couldn't answer that. All I wanted him to do was tell the truth.

To this he replied, 'I know how you must feel towards me and probably want to beat me up, I've been a real swine and deserve everything I get.'

My foot was in the door! Despite it being the end of his world, he remembered that he still had his bus money float on him, and he asked if he could take it to the main bus depot on Wilderspool Causeway. Phil was amazed when I agreed and I allowed him to go and do it and escorted him, minus handcuffs, so his workmates would not notice anything. We later interviewed him at the police station, and he admitted what he had done. I charged him with two counts of buggery and six counts of gross indecency. He wrote on the charge form 'I am sorry for all I have done'.

He later pleaded guilty, in Warrington Crown Court and received ten years' imprisonment. He deserved the ten years that he got, but it again put into perspective the weak sentence that Langshaw had received for abusing several dozen boys.

The police force doesn't have a union and the Police Federation is the nearest thing to it. My involvement was taking up more of my time; I had become a discipline representative and worked with officers who had been complained against. I was also the detective sergeant's representative for the county and chairman of the Sergeant's Branch Board. Each year we would go to a conference in one of the seaside resorts and there were periodic branch meetings. It was another interest, and I enjoyed the challenge. When I had joined however Mick Holland had advised against it and I had disregarded his good advice.

Chapter Thirty-Two

Police Federation Work and Discipline Duties

AFTER THREE YEARS AS THE Federation discipline rep, a case came my way involving a sergeant at Warrington with quite a few nasty complaints stacked up against him. He was a bluff speaking; old-fashioned sergeant by the name of Jockey Gerard and he was facing the sack. When the complaints were looked at carefully, they were minor, and I believed he was being treated badly. One of them was from a fellow woman sergeant called Denise Birchall. He had a quite justifiable grievance with her, and he approached her to make it. This developed into a slanging match, and she complained that he was bullying her. I questioned her motives – was she a sergeant or was she a woman? In these politically correct days gender should not matter. Two people of the same rank had had an argument, why involve the Complaints and Discipline Department? It was working on this complaint that I realised how the Cheshire C&D dealt with complaints. The woman sergeant later took the force to an Industrial Tribunal for discrimination in an unconnected allegation against other officers, including Ian Holding, the deputy chief constable. Oh, and the fact she must have been by-passed for promotion as she was a woman! no apology was made, and she retired.

By now the superintendent in charge was a woman, Ann Booth who I always got on well with and as a discipline rep I had a lot of dealings with her. Her immediate boss was Ian Holding, and he had the final decision; it was this man who directed how the job should be done. The morale in the force was suffering as officers had to constantly watch their backs. The most minor of complaints were, I felt, being treated in a draconian manner with little thought to what the officer had to put up with that led to the complaint. One of the complaints against a sergeant well illustrates this; I thought at first that someone was having a joke. He was the custody officer at Warrington. The post of Custody Officer is probably the most dangerous job in the force as far as attracting complaints is concerned. The pressure to do the job and comply with the amazing number of rules to 'ensure the welfare of the prisoner' means that it is a job that few sergeants want. This one was unique, he loved it!

One day a wild drunken thug was brought (or rather manhandled) in screaming and shouting. He was forcibly put into a cell and started to bang his head or something on the wall, at the same time shouting that he would make a complaint and say that the custody staff had battered him. Across from his cell was one of the interview rooms fitted with tape recording equipment for interviewing prisoners. During a routine fishing expedition by the C&D investigators it came to light that when this happened, the Custody Officer instructed a policewoman to prop open the door of the interview room and switch on the tape recorder. This would tape what the thug was saying and then, if he did complain, the evidence would be there to rebut the complaint. What a good idea, you may think if you are an ordinary sensible person; what common sense. Unfortunately, the words 'police' and 'common sense' are diametrically opposed, and he was accused of using a covert tape-recording device without the consent of a chief officer.

I had been introduced to the politically correct, morale busting new Complaints and Discipline Department under the overall control of Ian Holding the DCC and I did not like what I saw, neither did I like him. Unfortunately, I didn't make any secret of the fact and decided to work even harder on behalf of officers under investigation. Rightly or wrongly, I was never afraid of putting my head above the parapet and that still applies.

The sergeant never did get to a tribunal as like a lot of officers, the stress of the investigation made him ill, and he left the force early on a good pension. A good, strong sergeant had left the force in order that the weak, whinging variety could feel satisfaction. This practice of going off on the sick when under investigation has been criticised in the press and in a lot of cases rightly so, but officers under investigation are under extreme pressure. The internal investigation procedure has a lot to answer for. If the department simply dealt with genuinely corrupt officers, I would like to be on it. I hate corrupt police officers and believe that they should be dealt with far more severely than members of the public. If found guilty of a crime, they should be drummed out of the force and forfeit their entitlement to a pension. In certain serious cases, this does happen, but not often enough.

Whilst on the RCS I was told by an informant that a constable in the Greater Manchester Police was corrupt and running with the baddies. I delivered the informant to its Complaints and Discipline Department, now known as the Professional Standards Department, and sat with him whilst he made a statement.

This seems a good point to discuss what support junior police officers get from their senior management? Let's look at an example, a case that became known throughout the Cheshire Police as 'The Chester Four!'

A discipline inquiry involving four Chester constables was instigated by the deputy chief constable, Ian Holding, under his overall command. The inquiry had a very detrimental impact upon the morale of the force as a whole and lost to the Cheshire Police the services of at least one superb officer. What disgraceful deed had these corrupt officers done? Read on and make up your own mind!

A man had been stabbed in Ellesmere Port and taken to the Countess of Chester Hospital. He was found to have on him a small quantity of controlled drugs, enough only for personal use. The hospital staff handed these to his father, who believed at that stage that his son was dying. Quite properly he, in turn, passed the drugs to four police officers who were present.

What were they to do? The man was seriously ill. They weighed up the facts in a humane, common sense and caring manner and flushed the drugs down a toilet!

A sergeant became aware of their actions and reported the matter. The officers were suspended from duty and remained so for almost two years. All became ill with stress. Yes, they had carried out a misdemeanour but surely that should have been dealt with by way of a reprimand.

Not then in the Cheshire Police. They were charged with, amongst other things, 'Malfeasance in Public Office'. This offence alone carries a possible prison sentence.

Although not involved at all, I submitted a statement to the effect that I, like millions of others, had watched one of those fly on the wall police programmes when an officer doing a stop check had found a small amount of cannabis. In front of the camera, he had said that it was not worth bothering with and dropped it down a grid. Fortunately for him he was not in the Cheshire Police!

The legal proceedings continued, but simplistically. Two cases were discharged at the committal hearing; the other two attended Mold Crown Court and the judge threw out the entire case. He criticised the fact that it had been brought before him. The constables returned to duty, and despite one of them coming in the top 10% in the national sergeant's exam he decided that he would resign from the force. Surely this officer had far more to offer the people of Cheshire than the vindictive, office-bound senior officers like Holding, who used a sledgehammer to crack a nut in complete ignorance of the effect that it would have on force moral!

The case of 'The Chester Four' involves a sequence of events that must never occur again, but almost certainly will. Not by Ian Holding though, he died shortly after retiring.

I CONTINUED WITH MY FEDERATION WORK and prepared two speeches for the next National Conference. The first was to make it Police Federation policy to allow the licensing laws to be relaxed to allow pubs to open when they wanted and licence the licensee and not the public house. The second was to make it an offence to drink from an open alcoholic drink's container in a public place, a practice that was already banned in a hotch-potch way by various city and town councils. It meant doing a lot of research and speaking to the various interested parties, then presenting the finished product to the Federation Motions Committee who would decide which ones to allow to be presented at the Conference.

Both of mine were chosen, As Cheshire had not made a speech at Conference for longer than anyone could remember, I decided to allow one of the full time Federation staff to make one of the speeches and I would make the other. I stupidly gave him the best one!

What heavy drinking Federation rep wouldn't be happy with the pubs being open all day? At the conference I prepared to face the audience of thousands. I wore my cream summer suit especially. My sensible plea for drinking in public to be banned was soundly trounced. My other motion to allow the pubs to open when they wanted to, was passed with a massive majority, and became National Police Federation policy (a policy that conveniently disappeared when the law was actually changed to do just that, and they weren't sure if it would work). The speaker for my other motion was on a Radio 2 programme talking about my motion the next day but I was congratulated by a member of the Joint Central Committee. It was all good experience though. What argument could there possibly be for stopping people from drinking in public? The public disorder offences that would be affected would surely justify the law. But no, the Federation Conference was happy to allow pubs to stay open but not to stop people drinking in public. Now that pubs are allowed to open all day there has been mixed response, some good and some bad, but to be fair the bad (perhaps a little unfairly) has probably outweighed the good.

I can well remember the disturbances that would take place at the same time, 11pm, when all the pubs were forced to shut, but now the general bad behaviour of the younger members of the public has deteriorated to such an extent as to over-ride and abuse their right to 24-hour drinking. I believe that this is due to a total breakdown of respect for anything or anyone, mainly by the younger generation. The fact that our towns and cities have degenerated into hotbeds of anti-social behaviour has more to do with the mindset of a generation – pubs being open for as long as they want has had little effect upon this. They would just get legless even quicker if the pubs shut at midnight.

By now I had been voted Vice Chairman of the Cheshire Police Federation; the next step would be Chairman, which was a full-time post. It is to this end that I worked. The previous year, a half-hearted attempt had been made to produce a Cheshire Police Federation Magazine. It only lasted for two or three editions and was only small. I decided to re-introduce it, writing most of it myself. It would, I thought, be a good morale booster and a way of keeping the staff involved with what was going on. I could also give the readers a laugh. I was still a member of the HMS Bulwark Association, and they issued a small quarterly booklet, and I copied it. At first the new magazine was printed at great cost by the force, but after a while I managed to get the backing of Phil Williams, owner of Williams & Co. Insurance Management of Warrington who inserted some adverts and printed it themselves. It went well and had a circulation of about 1,500. The present Federation Magazine is in a far more professional format and quite informative.

Chapter Thirty-Three

Deputy SIO on a possible murder & Kidnapped girl

ON THE MORNING OF 8TH NOVEMBER 1998, I was called in early to deal with two prisoners arrested for a serious assault. The circumstances were that two lads had been walking through Warrington town centre late the previous night; they were themselves quite decent although one of them was a bit of a joker. They had come across two girls and the joker asked if they knew the meaning of the word 'mincers'. It was what they had been discussing between themselves. The non-joker of the two carried on walking, leaving his mate talking to the girls. He heard a commotion behind him and turned to see a rather thuggish male fighting with his friend. He started to walk back to break it up and, on the way, he had to pass through the assailant's friends. When he reached them, one of them, an eighteen-year-old, took a swing at him. The punch missed as he fended it off and he struck back with another punch but hardly touched him; certainly not hard enough to make any sort of a mark, and the man went down. In the words of the pathologist, he was probably dead before he hit the ground.

He was put on a life support machine, which after about two days was switched off. I attended the post mortem, which was carried out by a Home Office pathologist, and he found that the cause of death was what he expected. The carotid artery had ruptured at the base of his brain, causing almost instant brain death, and unfortunately it is quite common.

The DI had gone to deal with the death of a newborn baby found dead and abandoned near the Gulliver's World theme park in Warrington. He was later named Callum by police officers because he was found in the Callands area of the town. It was a long inquiry, and they weren't having much luck. There was an acting detective inspector in the office, David Blood, it must be said that by that stage, in my opinion, he was somewhat over promoted.

He was made Senior Investigating Officer and I was made deputy SIO. I told him that the town centre incident was an unfortunate death, but it was unlikely that proceedings would be taken against the men in custody. We had started what is known as a paper room, it was not a full-blown HOLMES inquiry, but was the next best thing. I interviewed the two men with another DS, and he agreed with me that they were telling the truth and the deceased was really the author of his own downfall. I released them on police bail. I then visited the parents of the deceased and they were understanding and fully aware that their son was no angel. I arranged a meeting with the CPS solicitors and told the David Blood that I intended recommending that no further action be taken against them. He disagreed saying that they, or at least the one who had struck the deceased, should be charged with manslaughter. We agreed to differ, but he insisted on coming with me. Although I was briefing the solicitor, he kept butting in and putting forward his point of view. What he was saying flew in the face of the available evidence.

The solicitor agreed with me and without the SIO being there, my recommendation would have been followed. The file was to be shown to the head of the Warrington CPS. Again, in view of the comments by the SIO (and to be fair one other solicitor had raised doubts about any decision not to charge them) it was sent for advice from a barrister. In legal jargon, it was sent to Counsel for advice. When this advice came back, it was in total agreement with my recommendations. Both lads were told that no further action would be taken.

Shortly afterwards I was contacted by an officer from the Metropolitan Police to tell me that an Asian girl had been reported missing. They suspected that her family may be involved, including a relative who was a consultant psychiatrist at what was then the massive Winwick Hospital near Warrington. He had a detached house in the grounds, and it was thought she may have been detained there. In this case the girl had acquired, to the disgust of her family, a black boyfriend.

I took some officers and a search warrant and went to the house; we were refused entry by the rather aged Asian Consultant Psychiatrist who we believed to be her uncle. The family denied any knowledge of her and when I insisted on searching the house, they weren't very happy, but it was a job that needed doing.

The girl was in the house and had been hidden from us in a bedroom, she was taken without complaint. After phoning to tell the London officer the news, he immediately set off to drive to sunny Warrington. He was over the moon and took the girl back with the intention of arresting members of her family. His team also went to deal with the uncle. Even though we had only rescued the girl I, as usual, made a full pocket book entry and this was fortunate as I was later called to the Old Bailey to provide evidence of her kidnap. In court my pocket book was carefully examined by the defence barrister. That was on a Friday and one of the other officers in my team had been warned to attend the following Monday.

When I told him that my pocket book had been examined, he laughed and thought that I was joking. He had not made a pocket book entry as he had just been there and was going to the same trial. A copy was made of my evidence, which basically was the same as his. In court when asked where his evidence was, rightly said that it was in my pocket book as we had compiled it together. They were found guilty of kidnapping.

Chapter Thirty-Four

Dealing with Rape Victims and Timewasters

THE DAYS WENT BY and on 3 January 1999 I was called in to work early because a rape had been reported. Two detective policewomen had gone out to interview the rape victim and her friend. The duty detective inspector was also called in. He was a young DI but very capable in the new school of policing.

We got the details over the phone. The two girls had been to the Mississippi Showboat Club in Warrington and one of the girls had met a man there who had raped her in an entry on a housing estate nearby. The DI and I went to the scene. It was properly cordoned off with an officer standing sentry. A used sanitary towel had been found and it was believed to have come from the rape victim. We had a good stranger rape here, I thought. Back at the office, DC Phil Hyde had traced the taxi driver who had taken the girls to the club. We went to see him.

'What were the girls like on the way to the club?' we asked.

He replied that they were 'a bit rough'. When asked what he meant, he replied that they had been talking about going and getting a man. They wanted one 'that potted the pink and not the brown'. To be honest, I had never heard the saying before, although it was obvious what it meant.

'Oh, that's not all,' he continued.

'Go on,' we prompted.

'I picked one of the girls up afterwards; she was with a tall lad with earrings in the top of his ears.'

When he gave us the description, it was obvious that he had picked up the raped woman and probably the rapist after the supposed 'rape' had taken place. This was not a pre-booked taxi; it was a complete coincidence. We were intrigued.

'What were they talking about?' we asked.

'Oh, about kids, he asked if she went to the Mississipi Showboat often and she said that she did, then he told her that he had an old black BMW car.'

'Did she sound upset?' we asked.

'No, not really, well, when he got out, she told me he was a bastard because he had torn her top, that was all.'

This lad had got out before her, paid the full fare for her to get home and left. Phil took a statement off him. The taxi driver had told us where he had dropped the lad off and we decided to start our search there. We started looking for an old black BMW and after a while we found it in the road outside a council house. We knocked on the door, looking for a lad over six foot tall with earrings around the top of his ears.

That same unmistakable person opened the door.

'Hello, we're from the police,' we said, wondering if he would kick off, but he thought for a second and replied.

'Oh, you've come about my shed.'

'What do you mean?' Phil asked.

'My shed, it was broken into last week,' he replied.

Phil told him that we had come about an incident the previous night and asked him if he had phoned a taxi.

'Yeah,' he replied, 'I didn't take someone else's cab, did I? I called on my mobile.'

This man obviously didn't know what we were talking about. Phil asked him what he did prior to that, and he said he had been to the Mississippi Showboat. By now it was getting a bit embarrassing, we were stood on his doorstep and his wife was probably in the house. Phil asked him if he really wanted to talk there.

'Oh, a bit confidential, is it?' he replied conspiratorially, 'I'll get my shoes.' He re-joined us and we sat in the car. We asked him if he had left the Showboat with a woman, and he said he had; we asked what had happened and he said that he had had sex with her. He said that he had been in the club, and she had been there with a mate.

'They wanted me to go home with them,' he said indignantly, 'but I'm a married man; I wouldn't do something like that!' He said that the woman had, at his request, started to give him oral sex in the alleyway when a man had walked past and it had made her jump. She had agreed to full sex and had pulled her knickers down. He had stood behind her and when he saw her large behind, he was repulsed and pulled them back up again, pulling them to one side and having sex with her. He was disgusted when he later found that she had been on her period and his underpants were soiled. In fact, he still had them on. He was arrested on suspicion of rape.

Before interviewing him, we had a meeting in the office. The two policewomen had returned and were present. I told them that we had arrested the alleged rapist and that he was a soft lad and it looked as if it would go nowhere. I read the statements that they had taken and there was nothing in the girl's statements about their conversation on the way to the club.

I told one of the policewomen to go and speak with the girl regarding their comments about 'potting the pink and not the brown'. She gave me a strange look and I pointed out that I had never heard that before. I also told her that she would have to tell her that if what the man said was true about that, and the oral sex, and taxi driver's claim that in the taxi after the incident it was unlikely that the CPS would even run it. She replied acidly that she had been with the girl for two hours and she could tell if someone had been raped or not. I told her that from what I had heard, the girl was a 'slapper'. At this she blew up again and stormed out of the room. I walked back to my office with the DI, and he shut the door behind us and said. I would watch her if I were you.

She came back without a retraction statement, and it was quite apparent that she had not even tried to get one. She did however apologise for her outburst.

The alleged rapist was interviewed and reiterated his story on tape. An advice file was submitted to the CPS with a recommendation for no further action. But because he had admitted having sex with her, the CPS decided to let the court decide. They added a rider that they assumed that the investigating officer had 'advised' the aggrieved of the possible result with such poor evidence. I had instructed her to do just that, but do not know or believe if she did.

On 14 December 1999, Phil Hyde and I were at Warrington Crown Court for the trial. As I have said, because the lad admitted having sex with her but denied rape, they decided to let the court decide, despite my recommendation that there was no case to answer. We were met by the prosecuting barrister whose first comments were to the effect of:

'Who is responsible for bringing this to court, it should never have got this far, it's a disgrace.' He went on to say that there was little chance of a conviction. Phil explained that it was against our recommendations and the CPS was to blame.

The alleged victim did not turn up.

The barristers met the judge, His Honour Judge David Hale, and he told them that he was unhappy with the evidence, and he had no intention of ordering her to attend. That day, local officers and Greater Manchester Police visited her at her home and the following morning she was collected by Warrington CID and brought to court.

Sitting in the witness room was the taxi driver waiting to give his damning evidence. His day was wasted; they never even got to him. The woman was the first in the witness box and, as anticipated by Phil, me and both legal teams (but not Crawshaw, the policewoman) was subjected to the most damning, embarrassing and upsetting cross-examination. A short way into this first cross-examination, Judge Hale stopped the trial, discharged the jury, and acquitted the defendant. I had been right. Had DC Elizabeth Crawshaw told the woman that the right course of action was a retraction statement then she would not have been worried for almost a year and she would not have had to suffer that horrible time in court. The defendant had also had his life turned upside down because of this.

Rape is a hot potato today, when a man is acquitted, the system is blamed, not the fact that there was no evidence. I have dealt with a few rapes and almost all went nowhere. In one, a woman had alleged that she had been gang raped by a group of men. They were all arrested and kept in overnight for me to deal with the next day. I went and saw the alleged victim with a policewoman. She had made it up completely. They had been nowhere near her. In a lot of cases that would be the end of it but on this occasion, I ensured that she was charged with wasting police time and, if my memory serves me correctly, she went to prison for a short while.

On another occasion I was called in early by a policewoman and investigated another report of rape. This time, the woman had had sex and had then complained, as she was frightened of her boyfriend. Another woman had been going home drunk and had gone into the bushes for a pee, fallen backwards into a stupor with her knickers around her ankles and come to later imagining the worst. All rapes are treated as serious offences, which they are. The genuine cases are horrendous, and the perpetrators deserve at least a life in prison but I'm sorry 'wimmin's libbers': most domestic ones are going nowhere and if the government changes the rules to make convictions easier there will be more than an acceptable number of miscarriages of justice. Police have in the past been criticised for putting women under pressure when they have reported a rape. After a TV expose this practice was curtailed.

Because now the police are expected to believe what the woman says and act upon it ruthlessly, more and more women have no doubt gone to court wishing that they had not reported it and have been put through an extremely stressful cross examination. Had a detective been allowed to say something like, 'Bloody hell love, there's not much evidence there you know, you may get hammered in court and he will probably get off,' it could be nipped in the bud.

But that is not to be. Once again, common sense has been turned on its head to the detriment of real rape victims!

My first experience of dealing with rape was back in my days as a plain-clothes officer. It was March 1977 when we received a report from the CID in Catterick to the effect that a group of squaddies had gang raped a seventeen-year-old girl. She had been invited back to the barracks by one that she knew and whilst they were in his room five of his mates came in and he left them to it. They all had sex with her against her will to varying degrees and at first the girl struggled and screamed and then, realising that she could not escape, she just lay still. Eventually the first man came back and told them to leave. We had to arrest one of the soldiers who was on leave in our area; we picked him up and asked him off the record if he had done it. He told us that he had done nothing but knew what had happened. As far as he was concerned, he had not touched the girl, we re-iterated that we were not bothered either way as we were not dealing and all he had to do was tell the truth. We took him to the police station and put him in a cell to await Catterick CID. When they arrived, we told the DS in charge what he had said. He walked to the cell door, opened the hatch, and said quietly:

'You know she had VD, don't you?'

The prisoner's face dropped, and he looked forlornly at the smiling officer. Within no time at all he had made an admission to taking part. He received five years in prison for his trouble, as did the others. The prosecution barrister in his summing up said the in a single mad hour they threw away their good character and their reputations for decency and humanity.

Shortly after in the later 1990s a new detective inspector was posted to the office, Ron Pearson, a gentleman, and a scholar, about as far removed from the likes of the one that was temporary DI and mentioned earlier, as it was possible to get. He had, during his short stay, done incalculable damage to the morale in the office and Ron was there to put it back.

We did one interesting job together during this time. The investigation into the death of baby Callum had been wound down after extensive enquiries and many suspects and witnesses had been interviewed. Any other information that came to light was to be dealt with by the divisional CID. When the police release details of a serious crime, there are always important pieces of evidence that are kept secret. This is to prevent the hordes of nutters and sad people who want to come forward and falsely admit to murders and suchlike from knowing the full story. In that way, they can be tested to see if they really have done it and quickly weeded out. The same applied to the death of baby Callum.

One evening we were on duty when a phone call came from a girl in tears. She was saying that Callum had been her baby and she had done away with him. I had one of the lads keep her talking and having traced the call sent DC Liz Crawshaw with another detective to the location – a phone box. The girl was still there and they brought her in. I decided that Liz and I would interview her – bearing in mind there was one crucial piece of information which was known only to the police. She was in tears throughout and we were both quite happy that she was the person we were looking for. When we asked her how she had done it, she told us a story that included the confidential piece of the jigsaw. That was enough for us, and she was arrested on suspicion of murder. We then contacted the DI who had been in charge of the inquiry, and he came over straight away. The girl's details were checked on the computer and, yes, she was known to be one of those sad individuals. Unfortunately, when she had been interviewed after giving herself up during the original inquiry into Callum's death, the interview team had inadvertently let slip all of the details, including the information we were withholding. Her past history was strewn with similar reports of her admitting things, all untrue. One day she will top someone and be told to sod off. The offence has not yet been detected.

Chapter Thirty-Five

Putting the World to Rights

UP TO NOW MY career had been relatively successful. I had been commended by the chief constables of Cheshire and Greater Manchester with many judges' commendations and letters of thanks. I had some regrets but most things that I had done, including during the dark days of the 1970s, I was proud of. I didn't like the way the force was going; political correctness had arrived with a bang and everyone had to be subservient to it. Policing, especially detective police work was changing, there was no room left for rule benders or as I was called in Crown Court one day, a Cavalier Officer. It was alright though because as the defence barrister said on his summing up:

'Do you, members of the jury, believe what my client says, or do you believe this officer with his cavalier attitude?' They believed me and his client went to prison!

Bosses like Mick Holland, Richard Hood and Frank Ball were a dying breed; they would be replaced with, in the main, back watchers and paper shufflers, obviously with some excellent exceptions. People who loved 'meetings' and who in the main were completely out of touch with the troops on the ground. The chief officers live in a world of statistics, policy, and advice.

A good example of this was the monthly Crime Policy meeting. As the Vice Chairman of the Federation and the detective sergeant's rep I would attend as the representative of the rank and file. On one occasion one of the esteemed leaders proposed that it was bad policy to bail suspected child abusers on police bail back to the house i.e., their home address without putting conditions on their bail. The detective chief superintendent seconded it and all around the table nodded sagely in agreement. When it got to me, I pointed out that, at that time, it was illegal for the police to do so and police bail could not have conditions placed upon it! After that the DCS looked to me for a nod in similar situations.

On Boxing Day 1999 I had the letter of the week in the Mail on Sunday (for which I won a computer) and it is even more relevant today. The scene is the parade room and a shift coming on duty is being briefed by the sergeant:

- **Sergeant:** Out you go, stop and search suspects after a mugging, question anyone who can help and arrest anyone that you genuinely believe to be guilty.
- **Constable:** What happens if one of them is from an ethnic background and complains of racism?
- **Sergeant:** You will be stopped going on patrol for months whilst senior officers investigate. You will lose overtime, probably two stone in weight through stress and possibly your wife. Friends back the complainant and it's your word against theirs… you stand a good chance of being charged and thrown out of the force.
- **Constable:** But what if we go out as little as possible, drink tea with old ladies, only talk to professional people, fill in forms when people are robbed and keep our heads down?
- **Sergeant:** No trouble, you'll be paid and promoted and go on telly and talk of empathy and understanding, even assure the public that the police are not afraid of doing their job.
- **Constable:** Thanks, Sarge!

Even very capable officers who have reached senior rank have a Sword of Damocles hanging over them. This is to ensure that if they want to go further, or remain in post, they must follow the mantra of political correctness. In the bad old days of the 1970s we did not recognise racism or sexism or any of the other myriad 'isms' that have been discovered since. We treated everyone the same, unless that is they gave us reason or suspicion not to, irrespective of their beliefs, race, God, or colour. Now these things take priority over real issues. That is why the public has a quality of life far removed from the flares and loud shirts of 1974. In the main they are financially better off but it doesn't take a government statistician to deduce from the fact that in 1974 we in the police had a very easy life, albeit a poorly paid one. Then consider that now the police are completely overworked. The reasons are many – there are far more dysfunctional families, single families and anti-social-behaviour, and there is no longer respect for the police on the streets or anyone else in authority for that matter. Above all they are swamped with needless paperwork imposed upon them by the government.

Chief constables, once all powerful and respected in their forces, have become poodles of the prime minister.

Towards the end of my service, I met officers in their first two years who could not wait for their pension! The morale is low and a recent survey amongst them revealed that a very high percentage would leave if they could get a comparable salary elsewhere. I'm not in it any more and can do my own thing. If it were 1974 again, I would join like a shot but it isn't, it's 2022 and the police service is entirely different. I wouldn't join now for a gold clock!

There are many things wrong with the police force of today and unfortunately there is little that can be done about it at local level. Most problems come from central government and chief constables bend over backwards to humour their masters.

Does it matter what race people belong to? In this day and age, it should be taken for granted that everyone is equal until proven otherwise by his or her behaviour. The current government is obsessed with racism and police forces ensure that they comply unquestioningly with every ludicrous diktat. Is it any wonder, with such an obsession, that experienced, courageous officers think twice before stopping someone from an ethnic minority?

You only need to look at the minutes of police management meetings – you'll find many are on the internet. You will be amazed, or perhaps not, when you see that many items on the agenda cover diversity, race relations, disability rights, transgender etc. Not a lot about clearing up crime, ensuring that the baddies fear the police, clearing the streets of dross and doing the police's job, not the social workers. These comments will be treated in the same way as similar comments made by a growing number of people from all walks of life who really are getting fed up with it all!

PACE, or the Police and Criminal Evidence Act 1984 – this wonderful Act that would prevent all the miscarriages of justice and all of the other bad practices that had got in the way of so-called 'Justice' – was hailed as the dawning of a new era in modernising police practices and deterring corruption. In reality it led to further prioritisation of the offender over the injured party and provided lawyers with unlimited opportunities to 'catch out' the police in their courtroom operatics. The police have always been in the spotlight of a critical press, legal system, and civil liberties lobbyists. This critique is done in the comfort of a safe environment when every action is carefully dissected and studied in order to find fault. Officers who, in the extreme heat of the moment must make an instant decision, can have their actions judged later over a nice cup of coffee and a biscuit. It is then decided that any wrong or genuinely misguided decision is dealt with in a most draconian manner. This is to ensure that backs are covered and in any possible future hearing, senior officers can say self-righteously that they took this or that form of action. The 'compensation culture' and 'lawsuit society' that we live in ensures police managers must watch their own backs. Accordingly, when all around them is chaos, the front-line officer has to think carefully before acting. But they don't have the luxury of time!

As previously mentioned, I was Vice Chair of the Cheshire Police Federation. This is the same organisation that is now supporting police officers in their aim to get compensated for falling over or tripping on kerbs. Can I just say that they, or at least the ones highlighted in the press, who apparently could not afford torches, are a disgrace and I would have been ashamed of wearing the same uniform as them. They are turning the police into a laughing stock, ably assisted by the Police and Crime Commissioners, like the one who engaged a silly seventeen-year-old girl as a 'Yoof Police and Crime Commissioner'. Who only lasted a short while.

It's perhaps wrong to criticise senior police management too much because it is a fact that the 'Blame Society' that we now have, leaves them genuinely vulnerable. Vulnerable to criticism and career drawbacks, that is – what a shame that this vulnerability is passed down to the front line to the detriment of the police's ability to effectively police. In those 'bad' old days of the 1960s and 1970s the officer who acted in good faith was supported from above. He was able to work without fear, but unfortunately this cannot be said today!

Let's look at the changing face of policing in this country over the years. What sort of police force does the general public want or what is feasible and what is not? We only have to go back to the 1950s and 1960s to see the type of policing that is perceived as the best. Those were the days of the British Bobby. The Dixon of Dock Green character that rode a pedal cycle, knew who all the rogues were and was always nearby when offences were committed. He did not have a radio to keep in touch, but there were unvandalised Police Boxes, later to be known as 'Tardises', which contained telephones. If he needed urgent help, he had his whistle and in the early hours he could always bang his small wooden staff on the footpath to alert other officers. There were far more constables per square mile than there are now, and the patrolling officer was a common sight.

These are the romantic memories of the British Bobby; a more detailed description has been lost in the mists of time. This is what people would like to see in place today, even younger people who could not remember those halcyon days know that this is what they want to see more police on the streets.

If we break it down a little, there were two types of policing: town policing and country policing. The specialist departments had little impact, there was a very small CID department who wore trilbies, but people somehow did not class them as policemen as the vast majority had no dealings with them. The police they saw in the street were uniform Bobbies.' In town the police were strict and respected, they were not subjected to quite the same violence as today and when they were, they did not treat the offender with kid gloves – nor were they expected to by either the general public or the offenders. In the country, policing was entirely different; the local officer really did know who the offenders were, not that there were many of them, and travelling criminals were almost unheard of. He would cycle round his large patch and stop to gossip. His job really was one of public relations and it worked. Things started to change in the 1960s with the introduction of more roads and road transport, when the police became more mobile. This was illustrated by such TV shows as Z-Cars. The CID started to become better known, as did the practices that they used. People had access to vehicles and so encountered the more overt Traffic Department.

It was true however that for some time to come only a very small majority had any dealings with the police. In the middle to late 1960s personal radios were introduced, the first introduction to modern policing. Police officers still carried out foot patrols and some of the working practices were still in the past. There was little change in the 1970s. The respect for the police was still there and the Bobby on the beat was still the best-known policeman. Crime was growing and the fighting of it was changing. Owning a television set was becoming universal and police programmes were a favourite. TV shows like The Sweeney were warts and all – before this, what the public did not know did not hurt them; now they were finding out and they did not all like what they saw. The public perception of the police was noticeably changing as the 1970s became the 1980s. From 1980 to 1990 the public view of the police service changed dramatically, gone was Dixon of Dock Green and Bobbies on bicycles two by two to be replaced by 'miscarriages of justice', car chases and the Police and Criminal Evidence Act.

The older generation started to reminisce about being given a clip around the ear by the local Bobby in a vain hope that those days may return. The genteel uniform consisting of a tunic, the trousers or skirt of which concealed a secret pocket that would take the police-issue small wooden baton and handcuffs were hidden away in an attempt to be as unprovocative as possible. Together with pro-active uniforms that openly displayed long, made for use batons, handcuffs and later CS gas and Tasers. Police were seen to carry guns on the mainland. Things would never be the same again. The assumption that the police did not tell lies or bend evidence had gone, the few corrupt police officers in a string of high-profile enquiries had cast a shadow over the police that will probably never go away. All this time, the Bobby on the beat carried on as best he could. He had to face a far more hostile public. Britain was no longer a no-go area for police assaults and the PC faced physical violence from offenders and public order situations alike. Even magistrates stopped believing the police as a matter of course.

Do we really need a uniformed presence on the street? This is now becoming a serious and much discussed question.

We have a Fire Service that sits in the Fire Station waiting to be called to a fire. With closed-circuit television cameras in all town centres, why can the police not do likewise? There is still a need for police patrol cars, that is not disputed, but what is being constantly questioned is the need for a foot patrol. Unfortunately, the arguments against foot patrolling police officers far outweigh the arguments for; there can be little argument for the need to provide a police presence in busy town centres, either during the day or night. Other areas are not as clear-cut. Police officers are no longer at the bottom of the salary league (neither are they near the top). They are paid for their knowledge and expertise, together with the work that they carry out. This work involves investigating, arresting, and interviewing suspects and completing and submitting more and more complex court files. It is work that requires people of a high calibre with above-average intelligence and training.

To have someone who fits these criteria walking around a housing estate or up and down a main road is a total waste of manpower and taxpayers' money. It is highly unlikely that anything will happen in his presence. The halcyon days of out-of-town foot patrolling are over. Now we have Police Support Officers as an alternative measure but the same applies to them. Let them walk around a council estate to humour the residents and be the butt of jokes for the badly brought up feral children, no other reason applies.

The new Police and Crime Commissioners may be a good thing if they get it right, but I hope I have explained how just putting Bobbies back on the beat is not the solution. Officers will have to work until they are older, and the Police Federation is squealing, 'How would you like to fight with youngsters on a Saturday night at 60 years of age?'

I have a simple solution. These days there are younger officers in office and in control rooms. Also, jobs on day work looking at projects and the like. Why can this work not be in the remit of the over 55s, so that there are more younger officers on the streets and less 60-year-olds fighting on a Saturday night? It would also keep officers working to at least 60 years.

Right, that is the police sorted, now let's get back to my story!

Chapter Thirty-Six

Guns and Goodbye

GUNS AND FIREARMS ARE THE bogeyman in the police vocabulary: to mention firearms is like invoking the devil. In the main, the job must be dealt with by trained firearms officers who, quite rightly, do everything by the book. There are many examples of firearms reports being treated lightly with dire consequences so now everyone, when the magic word is mentioned, backs off completely and calls in the cavalry. This happened once in Warrington when a man came to the desk to say that he had stopped at a traffic light and the passenger in the car alongside had a shotgun on his knee. Unfortunately, I couldn't hide quickly enough, and the station sergeant was able to slope it onto my shoulders. I asked the man if he was sure, it was a gun and he said that he was.

'Oh yes,' he continued, 'and I got his registration number!' Bang, the final nail was in the coffin of kicking the job into touch. I thanked him for his trouble and sent him on his way. No easy mark off that the car was circulated and could not be found. Now I had to do something, well, not me exactly, our esteemed firearms department so I pressed the button.

The car was traced to a house in St Helens, so now Merseyside Police would have to get involved as well. I met the teams at the smart detached house as they were setting themselves up. It was now dark, and the house was surrounded and then illuminated by powerful lights; normally the next thing is to phone up the suspect and ask him to come out.

He must not have been answering as a man with a bullhorn shouted at the house 'Armed police, come out and lie face down on the lawn!' All the neighbour's curtains were twitching as they climbed from their beds to have a look. The door opened and a man in his fluffy blue dressing gown and carpet slippers came out.

'Lie face down with your arms outstretched,' ordered the bullhorn and he did. He was quickly handcuffed, and I went to speak with him.

'Where is the gun that you had on your knee in a car in Warrington?'

'What gun?'

'We have had a report that the car in your drive had a man in the passenger seat with a gun on his lap.'

'That was me.'

'Got him,' I thought, 'God I'm good at interviewing!

'It wasn't a gun, it was my umbrella, would you like to see it, if that is what this is all about – I'm a bit annoyed to say the least.'

I viewed his black umbrella, brushed him down and cut off the plastic handcuffs, the firearms teams left to fill in the overtime forms and return to their beds and I went back to Warrington. Well, rules is rules!

Just to finish this tour through all that is good, bad, and crafty about the police, a story that is perfectly true.

Near Warrington there is the British Nuclear Fuels Limited (BNFL) plant at Risley; the nuclear industry has its own armed constabulary with similar powers to the British Transport Police, which are all police powers on or within a radius of their establishments. They were called the United Kingdom Atomic Energy Authority – or UKAEA – Constabulary, (in 2005 it was replaced with the Civil Nuclear Constabulary (CNC) But then in police parlance UKAEA was called the Ukulele Police. I was sitting at my desk one evening when I received a call from an inspector at Risley UKAEA explaining that earlier that day their chief constable, an ex-police superintendent, had called at Warrington police station. For some reason and in some way, he had perused the CID night book. This is the book in which the night CID officer record the night-time happenings. One of these happenings was a suspicious incident near to the Risley establishment (which is probably why he was there!).

It had been marked off in the official book with the words, 'The Ukulele police are dealing with it.' On seeing this his chief was none too happy and the inspector asked me politely if I could have words with the officer involved and forward a letter apologising for any hurt feelings. He would then pass it to the chief and we would all be friends again. I agreed and did what he asked, he was a very nice chap, and it was nice to help.

Life in the police was satisfying and most of the time it was fun. Being a detective was a great job with a good lifestyle, plenty of job satisfaction and the feeling that you were putting something into society. I also enjoyed my short time in uniform, I would perhaps have liked to have spent more time in it and progressed through the ranks but then again, that would not have been me. I enjoyed the cut and thrust of life on the front line and when I finally retired, I missed it – well, for a minute or two anyway. I would like to go through it all over again and would recommend it as a good career.

Saying that, those joining today join a very different organisation to the one I did all those years ago, and rather than say that it is not as good, I will say that it is different. The compensation culture and all that I have bored you with earlier does tend to take some of the fun away but then they can do things that I could not do when I joined. My first panda car was a Vauxhall Viva with white doors and a plastic box on the roof bearing the words POLICE. There were no blue flashing lights or two tones, the reason being that you had to be advanced trained to enjoy those luxuries, and then only in traffic cars. Now young panda drivers can rush around everywhere with blues and twos going, cutting a swathe through the busy traffic. There is not quite so much of the 'head for thinking, feet for dancing' mentality now so they can come to work, do their job, and go home. They also work far harder than we ever did and although they probably only receive half the respect, they can safely relax in the knowledge that they are helping society, even if sometimes it doesn't want to be helped.

Lightning Source UK Ltd.
Milton Keynes UK
UKHW010825250223
417650UK00001B/12